08524280MD

CM09924280

ABOVE AND BEYOND

STORIES AND REFLECTIONS FROM CHAPLAINCY AT HEATHROW AIRPORT

STEVE BUCKERIDGE

RITCHIE
CHRISTIAN MEDIA

ISBN-13: 978 1 914273 73 5

Copyright © 2024 by John Ritchie Ltd.
40 Beansburn, Kilmarnock, Scotland

www.ritchiechristianmedia.co.uk

All rights reserved. No part of this publication may be reproduced, stored
in a retrievable system, or transmitted in any form or by any other means –
electronic, mechanical, photocopy, recording or otherwise – without prior
permission of the copyright owner.

Typeset by John Ritchie Ltd., Kilmarnock
Printed by Short Run Press, Exeter

Contents

1. Please fasten your seat belts for take-off: an introduction ... 11

2. Why write a book?... 15

3. Our background.. 21

4. Just remarkable!.. 31

5. Twenty-four hours in the life of a chaplain 33

6. God at work even among tragic circumstances................... 39

7. Description of Heathrow... 43

8. The questions people ask!.. 47

9. Never work with animals or children?................................ 53

10. Nervous passengers... 57

11. Missionaries.. 61

12. Please ensure your own oxygen mask is fitted before
    helping others.. 65

13. Emergencies 71

14. Working with others... 75

15. Airport angels: a reluctant moniker.................................... 79

16. Mistakes and shortcomings.. 83

17.   The essence of presence: an example 87

18.   The essence of presence: the Biblical background............... 91

19.   The theology of Christian chaplaincy................................. 97

20.   The business of chaplaincy.. 103

21.   Practical models of chaplaincy 113

22.   Interactions with other works 119

23.   Epilogue – the journey 123

Doxa Theo

Looking out over Terminal 3, with the control tower and Terminal 5 in the background, as an aircraft takes off into the sunset

Flying over Heathrow (in a simulator!)

Judi and Steve in Terminal 5C

Steve and Judi in Terminal 4 departures

Please fasten your seat belts for take-off: an introduction

"Him who is able to do exceedingly
abundantly above all that we ask
or think"

(Eph 3. 20, NKJV)

It was a wet, grey, and thoroughly miserable early morning. I had a window seat and was headed home from an airport in northern England - but there wasn't much else to feel cheerful about at that moment.

I knew, however, that was all about to change. As the noise of the aircraft engines increased to take-off power, I started a timer as I anticipated one of my favourite experiences in flying.

It was less than two minutes later we broke through the gloom. Bright sunshine and blue sky. The clouds, increasingly far below, now a pretty, white vista.

As my journey continued, so did the improvement to visibility. At the highest altitude, the view was so good that the patchwork quilt of green countryside was a reminder that, from just a few miles up, perspective on the size of things on earth below is very different.

This is one of the ways that flying reminds me of faith. Rising above the clouds of difficulty, faith assures of things that are constant, and helps to keep the things of natural life in healthy perspective. But if all faith did was enable a temporary escape from day-to-day issues, it would be a helpful release - but short lived and ultimately futile.

Another remarkable aspect of flying is the ability to travel distances that for most of human history were either impossible or, until a few decades ago, would have taken many months. Amazing experiences – seeing the remarkable world in which we live, exposure to different cultures and climates, the ability to spend time with others - all come from flying and, with it, the knowledge that the horizon of our sight is not the limit of our travel.

Likewise, it is the ability of faith to go beyond the limitations of human view that is one of its greatest virtues. Just as with the natural horizon – where things seem to disappear, but we know that is entirely untrue - so faith sees beyond the illusion that death is the end. For me, the resurrection of Jesus Christ is the ultimate proof that there is existence after death, and that trusting the One who has come back to life to give eternal life, while very much an act of faith, is not unreasonable faith.

"**Above and beyond**" therefore seemed a fitting title for a book about flying and faith.

"Above and beyond", meaning putting in effort beyond what might be expected, also seemed fitting for chaplaincy. Chaplaincy has serving others at its heart, and I have seen many examples of chaplains who have gone above and beyond what might have normally been expected in their willingness to seek the good of others.

To the extent that it has been true in my life, it has been in response to the overwhelming grace of God that has truly gone above and beyond in bringing me into a relationship with Him and giving me the privilege of serving such a great God.

I hope that however you feel regarding flying, this book sharing some of my experiences of Christian chaplaincy at Heathrow will encourage you to think about faith. The faith that changes perspective on life to see it more from 'above' now, and with insight from the 'beyond' of eternity that is the future. And in whatever your sphere of service, I hope in some way it encourages you to go 'above and beyond' for the good of others.

2   2   2   2 ✈

Why write a book?

*"Encourage one another and build
up each other."*
(1 Thess 5. 11, ∩ET)

Primary reasons

My first reason for wanting to write this book was out of gratitude for the faithfulness of God. Time and again, God has guided our footsteps, given wisdom beyond ourselves and enabled us to be a help to people far more than we realised. I also wanted to share with you the encouragement that God is still at work. In a society that at times appears less religious than a few decades ago - and relatively few in the UK seem to show a deep interest in Christian things - God is still speaking to people!

The second reason was in appreciation for those who have practically helped and prayed for our work. There have been times when circumstances have been so remarkable, or God's help was known in a particular way, that I have come home and said, "I wonder who it was that was praying for us today?"! God knows those who have enabled the work to continue by their financial support. There have also been many who have shown an interest by their questions, asked for reports, and even given encouragement to write this book. It has been especially appreciated when close friends have, when necessary, affirmed gifting and given the courage

Above and Beyond

to keep going at times when humanly speaking it would have been easy to give up.

Thirdly, I wanted to contribute to the written literature that describes the way Christian airport chaplaincy is conducted – from both a theological and practical perspective. Many colleagues around the world will recognise plenty that is familiar in the stories that are told but the structures can vary surprisingly. The international nature of what we do means it is not always easy to 'pop down the road' and learn from chaplaincy elsewhere. If you are thinking of starting an airport chaplaincy, then some aspects will be of particular interest. In saying this, I appreciate a few sections may be of less interest to the non-chaplain reader – please skip a chapter or two if it helps you continue!

For readers where the details are not directly relevant to your sphere of service, I hope it nonetheless encourages you by the general sense that God works in varying situations, and imperfect arrangements – it is God's guidance that is the critical issue. In any sphere, we are unwise to wait until the ideal circumstances before stepping out in service (Ecc 11. 4-6).

Other reasons

If you are reading this as someone who is not a Christian, I hope this book will in some way direct you to Christ. I would especially encourage you to think about the greatest journey we are all on (that of our lives) – and, however far you get into the book, not to leave it without reading the concluding epilogue.

If you are reading this as a Christian, I hope it will encourage you in your service for God. It may be that there is an opportunity for chaplaincy and, just as I was encouraged by seeing airport chaplaincy in practice, so this may help you in your journey of discerning God's will.

But I have a more fundamental point in mind. I hope this book simply encourages Christians to get on with the work God is leading and equipping them to do. I knew very few airport chaplains when I started, and it is good to just have the confidence that God has placed us where He has - with purpose, gift, and opportunity to be used. Novelty for its own sake has limited value, but Biblical and Christian history has, I believe, plenty of examples of those who did a work for God being considered a bit odd or unusual. It does not matter whether others consider it conventional, controversial, crackpot, or cool – simply has God called to do it?

While chaplains may have a "job title", the majority of what I have done is simply being a Christian in a specific context. The guidance of God's Spirit, kindness to others, willingness to sympathetically walk with people in their difficulties, and speak of Christ as opportunities arise is very familiar territory to anyone with knowledge of the New Testament, and especially to those engaged in any form of pastoral work. In principle, I suspect the majority of what I am describing translates into many other areas of Christian work. The Bible speaks of Christians as part of a body and it is to be expected that, just as there are a variety of functions in our natural body, there will be the same principles worked out in the diversity of service seen in those in the church.

When researching how to write a book, I read one writer who said it was important to have a single key reason for writing. Having therefore failed at the first hurdle, I will keep going and say I hope there are reasons that are currently unknown to me. As with chaplaincy, and indeed wider service for God, the work is done and then the consequences left with a God who has plans greater than we can imagine. "Indeed, my plans are not like your plans, and my deeds are not like your deeds," says the Lord, "for just as the sky is higher than the earth, so my deeds are superior to your deeds and my plans superior to your plans."(Is 55. 8,9, NET).

Some caveats

I am mindful that a book on Christian airport chaplaincy touches on two distinct and specialist areas – those of theology and aviation. Both are similar in the sense of being 'heavenly' but are also alike in having their own distinct terminology, abbreviations and even idiosyncrasies! To have written presuming the reader had insight into both areas would have been to limit its perhaps already niche audience. I have therefore endeavoured to write assuming limited knowledge of either – while knowing it is likely that at least one of those fields may be familiar. I hope I have struck the right balance in the explanation of both.

The views expressed in the book are my own and do not necessarily reflect those of the Heathrow Multi-Faith Chaplaincy charity, Heathrow Airport Limited, the International Association of Civil Aviation Chaplains, or any church with which we have been associated.

The book is written from a Christian perspective, reflecting my own beliefs and convictions. Heathrow operates a Multi Faith Chaplaincy with chaplains from the six major faith groups of the UK on the team. The chaplains will seek to help all, irrespective of the person's beliefs (or even absence of faith). Colleagues within the Heathrow team, and more widely, often hold different views to my own.

In operational environments, policies and procedures change over time and a narrative of how something was done historically may not reflect current practice. Most of the book is UK based and, while I very much hope it will be of interest to international colleagues, the applicability may vary.

There are times when a little literary license has been used. This is just because my shift notes (or memory!) did not have the incidental details that help make a book more interesting. That said, all the stories are based on real experiences.

I have intentionally used no names to protect people's privacy. Appropriate confidentiality is a key part of chaplaincy, and I wanted to avoid any impression that a private conversation with a chaplain might one day find its way in an identifiable form into a future publication.

Acknowledgements

My wife Judi is the exception to using a name in the book. I am truly grateful for her in all that we have endeavoured to do in our service for God in chaplaincy and more widely. She has been a volunteer with the Heathrow Multi Faith Chaplaincy team since 2017 and there have been many interesting shifts we have done together. We talked about whether the book should be co-authored - as many of the incidents reflect our shared experience – but found that a bit unwieldy! So, although the book has been written by me, it reflects a joint work in which we are very much both engaged. Judi has also kept my more anorak aviation tendencies in check, for which no doubt fellow chaplains and readers are glad!

Our four children have all embraced an association with aviation throughout their lives. They have happily flown to all manner of places and their confidence around airports and desire to embark on their own adventures has been a joy to witness. Even more, has been the way each in their own way has developed a caring spirit for others that is at the heart of chaplaincy. Thank you for when you accepted the occasional intrusion into family life that the chaplaincy work has brought – and the times we helped people even when on holiday! Mum and I pray you will all use your many capabilities to be a blessing in your own areas of service for God.

We have appreciated serving alongside fellow chaplains too numerous to list. There has been guidance, support (particularly in the tough times) and a sense of camaraderie that has made the work much more enjoyable. It is also a privilege to serve alongside so many professional colleagues at Heathrow and more widely in aviation.

To our many Christian friends who have prayed for and asked after the work - it is appreciated. My particular thanks to K, S & P (you know who you are!) who in your specific and important way have been such a significant encouragement to keep going with chaplaincy. The Lord knows the impact that those 'behind the scenes' have had in the incidents in this book even taking place.

We are grateful to Lord's Work Trust in Scotland for all their help over the years and their willingness to be so encouraging and practically helpful in the publication of this book.

3   3   3   3   ✈

Our background

"He has done all things well."

(Mk 7. 37)

Steve

I grew up just north of Heathrow airport. Home, primary school and the church building we regularly attended were all under the approach to runway 07 at Northolt aerodrome, and my secondary school sport pitches also looked down onto that airfield.

Dad was an airline pilot, and my first flight was with him on the flightdeck of a Hawker Siddeley Trident to Glasgow at the age of seven. I only remember a few details about that flight – one of them being gently told by another of the pilots that I needed to be quiet for a minute as "Daddy was busy". Perhaps the ability to talk in an aviation context had early origins! This trip started a tradition of birthday treats: an annual trip with Dad, often for night-stops in Europe. As this was before the restrictions that followed the September 2001 terrorist attacks, I was able to be seated on the 'jump seat' with the pilots. The learning, inspiration and insight into airline crew that came from doing those trips has always stayed with me. Aberdeen, Dublin, Berlin, Helsinki, Madrid, Lisbon, Stockholm, Copenhagen, and Jersey all hold memories.

Not that God's preparation was merely exciting trips around Europe! There were some poignant memories that, looking back, were far more significant than I appreciated at the time. We were away on holiday in August 1985 and listening to the news on the car radio. The awful "Juliet Lima" tragedy at Manchester was the leading story. A Boeing 737-200 had a technical issue with one of its engines resulting in an explosion during take-off and 55 people died. Dad had recently converted onto this aircraft type with a closely connected airline and would regularly fly in and out of Manchester. While flying is incredibly safe, I have never forgotten what it is like to wonder how close a relative has come to being involved in a major incident.

In December 1988, one of my brothers was due to go to Dublin for his birthday flight. He was unwell and I remember cheekily asking if I could go instead. (He has always been very gracious about me stealing that trip; his interest in aviation is a little less than mine!). It was an early flight back the next day and I recall waiting in the hotel lobby as the crew assembled. There was some hubbub of discussion about the previous night's events – Pan Am 103 had been blown up over the Scottish town of Lockerbie after leaving Heathrow bound for New York. In those early hours after the event - when emergency response was still taking place and definitive information on causation was not available - I have always admired the quiet professionalism of the crew in the way they reacted to what is still the worst aviation incident in UK history. Without drama, and even when out of the public eye, they went about their preparations clearly very aware of the significance of the event and the impact it could have on passengers, but with a commitment to doing their job well.

While some parental time away is normal for many families, another feeling I still remember is how it felt as a child to look forward to the return of a travelling parent. Mum did the job of looking after us as children without the benefit of modern technology - three rings on the landline phone would be the indication that Dad had arrived. On one occasion we had the news that a baggage truck had hit the engine of Dad's aeroplane while it was parked in an overseas airport. The passengers were put on other flights, but the pilots stayed for a couple of extra days while a repair was carried out and the aircraft brought back to London as a ferry-flight. I appreciate that modern technology means aspects of this are different today but I still have empathy for those – especially young people – coming to meet someone who has been away.

Pilots are incredibly well-trained, practising every 6 months events they will in all probability never carry out in real life. The benefit of a checklist, repeatable processes, clear communication, and the priority of safety influenced my upbringing in a positive way.

A favourite memory is of Saturday afternoons cycling into the airport with Dad, briefing for whatever flight he was doing, and then watching his departure from the spectators' area on top of the Queen's building (since demolished to make way for Terminal 2 / The Queen's terminal). A happy hour or two would then be spent exploring the Central Terminal Area and (especially if the weather was cold) watching aircraft from the view over the Bravo cul-de-sac (as it was called) from inside Terminal 1. These days the ability to give passengers directions anywhere in the airport is not easy to pass on to new chaplains when it appears God started my preparation by many hours spent exploring Heathrow back when I was a teenager!

Gaining Bible knowledge was a crucial part of my teenage years with a weekly Bible study for young people and plenty of other good teaching being invaluable. While it required some hard work at the time, now looking back I particularly appreciate that it was done in a way that encouraged personal study of the Bible. Aside from helping with all the questions we are asked as chaplains and being preparatory for contributing for many years to the staff Bible study, this has been key in laying a sound foundation for the wider work of teaching the Bible among Christians. There are few joys greater than seeing Christians growing in their enjoyment and understanding of Scripture, and when I now have the privilege of seeking to explain divine truths in an encouraging and practical way, I recognise the influence of those formative years.

An economics degree at Cardiff meant having time away from the Heathrow area. The only memories I have of a Saturday afternoon visit to Rhoose airport are being stuck behind a tractor for most of the drive there and seeing a solitary aircraft take off! I'm pleased to say my view of Cardiff aviation was somewhat redeemed by finding a fellow student who was a pilot and going for a flight together a few months later. It has also been a useful memory to help with empathy for passengers who may have only previously experienced smaller regional airports before coming to Heathrow.

Eleven years were spent with British Airways, mainly in safety, including being a safety manager when Terminal 5 was being planned and opened. There then followed four years with airside operations within Heathrow. This not only gave a solid knowledge of the airport in terms of layout and processes but, perhaps more importantly, of the many people who work at Heathrow.

Judi

Judi's childhood was different. She has never had the same technical interest in civil aviation as I had - and would maintain that is not a bad thing! Home for her was relatively close to Fairoaks airport and she has memories of being taken by a grandparent to watch the aeroplanes with her cousins.

Both of Judi's grandfathers were employed within aviation. One worked for the RAF and told stories of the antics youngsters would get up to in days when security was much less strict than today. The other designed and made tools at Brooklands aircraft factory when Concorde was being produced. Perhaps there was something in the genes after all!

When we met, Judi's only flying experience had been on a small aircraft undertaking a sight-seeing tour - and it had not been the happiest of trips! I was keen to see if aviation would be a joint interest and so a few months into our relationship I organised a birthday shopping outing – a day trip to Edinburgh, on a much larger aircraft, courtesy of staff travel. So far as we recall, it went well from a flying perspective - though I do not think either of us could have envisaged that twenty years later, Judi would be confidently directing people around Heathrow.

Judi's background is in childcare and development, and her ability to quickly build rapport with children, especially those with extra needs, has often been useful in helping families through the airport. Indeed, within a few weeks of being fully appointed as a chaplain she was given an award for help given to a family – something she is always happy to remind me about!

College projects that required creativity and design have been helpful in producing visual exhibition material for the wider schools' work we do and for some design work within the chaplaincy.

In recent years Judi has been undertaking studies in Biblical counselling. This seeks to use the Bible and prayer as an integral part of helping people with the problems and issues of life. As with many pastoral situations, we do not attempt formal counselling as part of chaplaincy, but skills such as careful listening and walking empathetically with people in their varied experiences are similar. Developing greater capacity to frame conversations in a way that encourages others to be honest about their fears and failures, along with confidence to pray with people in all sorts of situations have been positives from these studies. This is clearly useful within chaplaincy but also more widely in seeking to be available for others

- especially those dealing with the variety of mental health related issues from which Christians are not immune.

A theme in Judi's background before becoming a chaplain was helping others. This started at a young age and was even commented on in a school report! Once she was driving, there were many times she made a point of being available to transport others and this was instrumental in us meeting. When our children were at home, we both made career sacrifices, and Judi especially so, believing that parenting is one of the most challenging and important jobs God ever entrusts us to do. I have lost count of the times when, often at short notice, a bed has been made ready or a meal prepared as that sacrificial care for others has continued!

Judi does not have as much aviation in her background, and in a sense, we illustrate two different ways in which God works. Sometimes it is obvious how over many years He has been preparing for a particular sphere. Other times, God takes a willingness to step out of our 'comfort zone' and uses our attitudes and abilities in a less expected way. Both require a dependence on God and have their specific challenges.

Together

More significant than our aviation connections have been the spiritual heritages we were blessed with. We both grew up in Christian homes where there was a desire to put God first, read the Bible, pray, reach others with the gospel and be hospitable. Love, stability, and a measure of healthy discipline were considered 'normal'.

Not that we would want to give any impression that we were perfect children or had perfect upbringings. As with church life, marriage, and now our own family, we have come firmly to the recognition that something lacking perfection is no reason to ignore the blessing it may also be. It is truly amazing the way God is the master at working in the imperfect and we are grateful for all that was good in the foundations laid in our lives.

And in the matter of personal faith, upbringing was of course not enough. In God's grace we both placed our trust in Christ at a young age. Through different verses in the Bible, we appreciated we were sinners who needed Jesus Christ to save us. By faith in Him and the work He did in His death and resurrection we were saved out of that perilous position and given the wonderful gift of eternal life. Since those experiences of conversion, we have both endeavoured to live for Him. We were subsequently baptised and became members of local churches as teenagers. This happened at different times and circumstances with God speaking to us through different parts of the Bible, but the result was the same – at conversion we were born again into the family of God and by the time we met, we had independently made significant decisions about wanting to live for God.

Once the relationship between Judi and I was serious, there was agreement that when the Lord called, we would be willing to leave full time employment and give as much time as we could to serving God. We considered some overseas missionary work but were particularly concerned about the significant spiritual need in the UK.

We were engaged in March 1999 on a boat during a daytrip to Geneva. Arrangements had been made for us to spend the whole of the return flight on the Flight deck, but chaplain diplomacy will prevent any comments about whether this was the best bit of the day. To finish off the day we took the train across to Terminal 4 and had a celebratory smoothie in the Hilton hotel (in those days it was the only hotel connected to a terminal).

We were married the following year (the suggestion of using the Heathrow Chapel never made it past the 'look that says it all' stage) and unfortunately (in my mind anyway) the planned going away in a helicopter was deemed unfeasible due to a certain airport's proximity. For our honeymoon we flew for the only time in my life out of the old terminal 2 at Heathrow, though I'm pleased to say there were other reasons for it being memorable.

A few years later, during a visit to see friends in Canada, we had our first introduction to chaplaincy. The airport at Winnipeg may not share too many similarities with Heathrow but it was there that we saw airport chaplaincy 'up close' for the first time. Several Christians we knew were involved, and a long-term consequence of the work they were doing there was to plant the seed in our minds concerning this work. It was a joy some years later to spend a day shadowing one of their team in their new terminal and exchange experiences. One common characteristic between the work there and what we are doing now – and which applies in so many aspects of serving God – is that He is often using us is ways that were not obvious at the time, and we will always be grateful for the inspiration that work was to us.

In 2012, there came the culmination of many years of God's leading and the clear guidance that this was the time to leave full-time employment to embark on our next phase of Christian service. We believe that this was specifically in teaching and preaching the Bible, working with young people particularly in connection with schools, and a few months later, there also came the opportunity for Steve to start volunteering with the Heathrow Multi Faith Chaplaincy team.

God specifically encouraged us in the early part of that year before taking this step of dependence on Him by the words in Genesis 50. 21: "Do not be afraid; I will provide for you and your little ones". As with any work for God, sacrifices have had to be made and we would not profess to have always understood why God has chosen to do things in the way He has. However there have been many stories of His remarkable provision and we are grateful for those who have been prompted by the Lord to help practically.

Looking back, it would have been impossible to have designed life the way it has turned out, or realised at the time that events took place, the purposes God would have. There are times when God was allowing experiences that - in some case decades later - would be seen to be useful in preparing for subsequent service.

If today your current circumstances seem difficult, unusual, or even humdrum, I hope you can take heart from our stories. Our very ordinary lives have illustrated to us that God is not casual in his activity and our imagination is often not good enough to contemplate what He has in mind from the experiences we are passing through. So often we want to know in the moment the reason why God is doing something - but He does not owe us explanations. He is wanting our faith in, and does not need our endorsement of, His design. Even in our limited experience, there are sufficient times when we can look back and see that God knew what He was doing so that we can have confidence that in eternity - when we can truly see and understand the big picture - we will say, "He has done all things well." (Mk 7. 37).

Just remarkable!

"Wonderful are Your works."

(Ps 139. 14, NASB)

Walking our children home from school may sound a strange place to start an airport chaplaincy encounter. However, one Monday afternoon when the children were little and we were nearly home, a car came into a parking space outside our front door. The lady driver was clearly flustered, and a tense conversation was taking place with the male passenger. We enquired as to whether they needed any assistance - and it transpired they were father and daughter on a long journey from west England into London.

They were completely lost, but after a while we established they had come off the nearby motorway a junction earlier than they had intended. We calmed them down, gave some simple directions and they went on their way happier than when they had arrived.

We continued our day and didn't give it much thought, other than a brief conversation wondering whether with such a specific encounter we should have used it to give a little direction to spiritual things. We are often reminded that these things do not need to be forced and, much as there are times when our lack of courage or imagination may unnecessarily keep us quiet, God's timing is also the best.

Three days later I was in Terminal 2 departures and, having passed through security, found myself in a significant crowd, overlooking the shops below. Out of the corner of my eye someone caught my attention, and I recognised the lost man from earlier in the week.

"Hello again," I said, "did you find you way okay? And did you and your daughter make up on the journey?"

The man was stunned to the point where initially he didn't know what to say. Once he recovered, it transpired he had even more reason to be surprised than I supposed. He was flying to New Zealand but had been having several issues with his journey. This included his original ticket being changed from a Gatwick departure to Heathrow, and the day of travel having been altered meant he had never planned to be where he was.

He looked me in the eye and said: "It must be that God intended me to meet you again. What message do you think he wants me to hear from you?"

I confessed I didn't know enough about the man's circumstances to be able to say anything specific, but I assured him there is a message that God wants us all to hear. I gave a simple explanation of how the Bible says that God, in amazing love provided Jesus Christ to save us from the consequences of the wrong we have done. Through His death and resurrection those who turn from their wrong and put their faith in Christ will be forgiven and have everlasting life. The man listened carefully, thanked me for my help and went on his way.

It defies human explanation that God could arrange our circumstances such that at the right time someone would be put outside our house for us to show a little kindness - and then a few days later their plans be changed to put them next to me in among the teeming thousands at Heathrow. Much as I enjoy explaining the good news of the Bible, there is also nothing like seeing God at work, doing what in human ability we could never do. God clearly speaks into people's lives as He works to bring them to Himself.

Twenty-four hours in the life of a chaplain

I t is rare that all the interesting things happen in one go, but this was a genuine 24-hour period that happened while I was writing this book.

1230   *Airline Christian fellowship group for staff:* time of prayer and discussion around the Bible. One participant has recently had a medical diagnosis and is awaiting more news on the treatment options, another doing a temporary job in the hope something more substantial will materialise. The weekly bulletin I write goes out to many more than come to join us, and includes a thought from Scripture. During the afternoon I exchange messages with those in different parts of the world who had been unable to come on this occasion

1830   *Both head into the airport to meet a colleague.* Judi is going to meet a flight at the request of the Red Cross where refugees are arriving to join a family member who is already here. The refugee mum is travelling with several children, and it is difficult to imagine the circumstances they are leaving, but also the feelings that must go through their minds coming to a completely different country. We go for coffee to talk through the best way of handling the situation.

1915 *Bump into a PEM* (Passenger Experience Manager – colleagues who are operationally responsible for the smooth running of the terminals) and discuss how an ambulance has been requested by the flight the refugees are on. They also mention a serious incident that has happened in another terminal. A staff member has gone to hospital – although we do not need to take any immediate action we will let the rest of the chaplain team know so those in that terminal over the next few days can be alert for staff who have been affected by it.

1955 *Flight arrives and refugee family identified.* Medical issue does not need chaplain assistance. Family speak no English and cannot easily read their own language – online translation is again a boon!

2020 *Judi calls Steve to go and speak with the refugees' relations* who are waiting in arrivals. Border Force were also in contact seeking to establish various matters before the family are allowed to enter the UK.

2050 After watching the family reunion, *a lady in her late thirties asks for help.* She was concerned for her husband. Their history is complicated. She has lived in the UK for many years but now has a disability that means, having been at the airport most of the day, she could do with going home to take some more medication. Her husband has not visited the UK before. Judi provides her with some food and drink, and I and our colleague cross back though security and find a senior immigration official to see if there is any information they are willing to share about the case. Turns out Border Force will not be making a quick decision, and we agree that it would be of minimal benefit for the wife to remain at the airport. We advise her to go home and call back in the morning.

2130 *In walking through the baggage hall* it has become obvious that there is a lot of activity around a baggage belt. A late-night Airbus A380 has 'gone tech' - there is an issue with the aircraft such that it cannot be quickly fixed, and the passengers will be accommodated overnight in local hotels. The small number of staff are almost overwhelmed by the unexpected crowds.

The three of us offer our services to the airline manager who is walking about with a phone almost permanently attached to her ear. The extra assistance and first-class passengers have been helped, and we move to an area of the departure's concourse where the remainder of the passengers are patiently waiting. We arrange some water to be brought and give some presence of mind to the staff who, as fast as they can, are allocating several hundred hotel rooms.

We mingle among the passengers, explaining, calming, reassuring. Someone says they are glad to see us and explain they are Christians who live a few miles away. It turns out we have some mutual friends and can share some encouragement together. They end up being one of the last to be finished and so we accompany them to their hotel and pray together in the reception area.

This happens to be the Hilton hotel in Terminal 4 where we ended our engagement day, and the date today is a day often thought of as romantic. We smile at the amusing coincidence but as it is heading towards midnight, decide that we are too old for celebrations at this time of night and head home. It would be tempting to not set the alarm but I am on call tomorrow and if there is one thing worse than being woken up by an alarm, it is being woken up by the phone ringing and seeing it is an airport number!

0737 *Airport control ring* to say a flight that landed an hour ago has had a death on board. Breakfast becomes grabbing a snack and, with a prayer to ask God to keep me going, I head back to the airport.

Details are a bit scarce, and it becomes apparent this was a "no notice" event. Sometimes we receive a few hours' warning that a medical event has happened on board. But in this instance, it is not until after landing that the relative travelling with the now deceased passenger had gone to wake them up and found them unresponsive.

The police are undertaking interviews with both the relative and crew. At the end of a long overnight flight, everyone is tired and there was little the crew could have done. One of the crew says they are a Christian and we talk about the way Jesus cared for Mary and Martha in John chapter 11. In that Biblical event so often turned to at times of bereavement, they had their questions but there could be no doubt about Christ's love for them.

The police take their time probing a variety of angles as I sit with the relative. I know from my experience in safety that it takes a lot of patience to think rationally and comprehensively when questioning someone who is emotionally involved in the events. The staff arrive for the departure flight and calls are made to ensure the passengers will not be sent to the gate until the aircraft is ready.

The police decide it would be prudent to look at the checked-in baggage of the deceased and so I accompany a couple of officers and the relative through immigration and into the baggage hall. I find a quiet area and we have the somewhat surreal experience of opening the cases.

Some more relatives are waiting in the public part of arrivals and after the tears of reunion in such a sad situation, there are questions they ask me about the future. They also ask about my role, and it gives opportunity to speak briefly on spiritual things and offer to pray. One family member is particularly keen for this and takes hold of my hand as I pray for God to help them in the days ahead.

Walking to the car park there is a discussion as to quite where they parked their car! Fortunately, they see the funny side of this and helpfully acknowledge that, even in grief, it is not wrong to keep our sense of humour. I assure them that even on the best of days, it is surprising how similar different levels in a multistorey car park can look! I arrange for their car parking fee to be waived and make sure they exit the barriers without any issues.

Returning to the terminal building, I make a visit to the management offices of the airline that was involved. This is the second similar incident they have had in the last few weeks, and a senior manager wants to review how it has gone. There is some discussion about a chaplain talk at a future team event.

I send a message to the chaplain at the airport the inbound flight came from, as I had given their details to the crew.

1330 *Head round to Terminal 5 for hopefully a quiet afternoon* of writing up the day's events.

God at work even among tragic circumstances

Jesus answered him, "What I am
doing you do not understand now,
but afterward you will understand."

(John 13. 7, ESV)

Walking into the prayer room above Terminal 3 arrivals, I was immediately aware of a lady sobbing. This was early on in my chaplaincy experience and one of the first times I would be faced with the rawness of grief that is present in the immediate aftermath of sudden death. The passenger had just returned from Australia after a visit to a terminally ill relative. Now on arrival she had been surprised by the absence of their father who had agreed to pick her up. His military background meant he was known for punctuality. A concerned call was made - and sadly the gentleman was discovered dead in his garden.

I offered to make phone calls and stayed with her for a couple hours until her husband arrived. As we discussed a variety of things including some quite specific spiritual matters, she asked who it was had called me, or how I knew that she was in the prayer room needing help. She couldn't understand when I said that nobody had sent for me.

"It is too big a coincidence," she said, "how do you explain you being here?"

I pulled out my phone and showed her the message I had been reading as I approached the prayer room.

Judi had written, "Just praying that you'll meet someone you can help."

A week or two later a card arrived. In among the appreciation for the care shown, was a simple statement:

"You said things about God that a colleague has also been saying to me recently."

It had been one thing to be "in the right place, at the right time" – that is hard enough to explain. But then to discover that one is part of a seemingly infinite jigsaw puzzle of the divine working in an individual's life is truly thrilling.

God's work is often described as "links in a chain", and it can be tempting to want to be something more. With a little thought comes the realisation that it is a deep privilege – and almost breathtakingly exciting - to just be any part of the divine plan.

Many years ago, I asked a godly aunt – whose prayers and occasional advice were formative in my early Christian development – to tell me her favourite hymn. She had quietly influenced many people for good, and took me to this 18th century hymn that includes the verses:

> *Father, I know that all my life is portioned out for me;*
> *The changes that are sure to come I do not fear to see:*
> *I ask thee for a present mind, intent on pleasing thee.*
>
> *I would not have the restless will that hurries to and fro,*
> *Seeking for some great thing to do or secret thing to know;*
> *I would be treated as a child, and guided where to go.*
>
> *I ask thee for the daily strength, to none that ask denied,*
> *A mind to blend with outward life, while keeping at thy side,*
> *Content to fill a little space, if thou be glorified.*

The words were written by Anna Waring from Neath, South Wales who spent her time quietly visiting prisons to witness to those there. Perhaps today she would have been called a chaplain.

It is one thing to praise God when He is at work in the good times. Life is going smoothly. Things are working out as we planned them. It is quite another to rest content when the opposite is true. God does not promise to take the problems away. But the noticing of how He is still at work I have found is all it takes to be reminded that, although we may not currently understand why God is doing what He is doing, it is enough to know that it is God that is doing it. And He can be trusted.

7　7　7　7 ✈

Description of Heathrow

"For God so loved the world"

(Jn 3. 16)

I am including here a basic outline of Heathrow. These details are not comprehensive but may be helpful in describing the general context of the chaplaincy work.

There are 4 terminals, two of which have satellite buildings:
Terminal 2 A & B (opened 2014): A & B are connected by a walkway under the "Kilo" taxiway.
Terminal 3 (opened 1961).
Terminal 4 (opened 1986).
Terminal 5 A, B & C (opened 2008): A, B & C are connected by the Track Transit System or TTS, an automated train-like vehicle that operates under the "Alpha", "Bravo" and "Charlie" taxiways.
(Terminal 1 was closed in 2015).

All the terminals are connected within the secure area of the airport by a bus network.

The "Central Terminal Area" (CTA) comprises Terminals 2 & 3 and there is a public walkway between those two terminals. The CTA, Terminal 5, and Terminal 4 all have bus and coach connections, a tube/metro station plus a main railway station and are therefore also well connected by public transport.

There is a variety of ancillary buildings used by staff, a large Cargo area and several office buildings. A total of over 1300 take-offs and landings take place each day on the two pieces of two-mile-long tarmac that comprise the 09L/27R and 09R/27L runways.

Around 80 million airline passengers pass though Heathrow each year and, at particularly busy periods, more than a quarter of a million of them come through in a single day.

Heathrow is a hub airport and a key consequence of this is that many passengers do not have London as their destination - approximately one third are transferring onto another flight. When combined with being a multi-terminal airport, this gives specific characteristics to the chaplaincy work. Inter-terminal transfers that become short on time for example (perhaps because of a delayed in-bound flight reducing the time available to do the connection) can be an opportunity to stay with a passenger and calmly go across the airport. Missed connections can become difficult where the individual does not have a right of entry into the UK or have none of the items for an overnight stay in their cabin baggage.

Another characteristic of being a hub airport is the mix of short-haul and long-haul flights with passengers travelling on anything from a 40-minute domestic flight to a 17-hour intercontinental route.

The industry is continually changing but historically Heathrow had a significant proportion of business / premium travellers. The mix with leisure travellers has implications for some of the facilities provision (such as lounges) and the level of familiarity those flying have with the airport – which in turn impacts on the questions passengers ask and needs they have chaplaincy wise.

The airport is not all about passengers - Heathrow is one of the largest providers of employment in the local area. This is comprised of those employed directly by Heathrow and those employed by companies operating at the airport. There are also jobs connected to the airport but where the person may not be geographically at the airport, or those who come temporarily through the airport because of the nature of their employment (flying or using public transport as part of commuting, crew based elsewhere, and those on short term contracts for example).

Spiritual issues transcend all these divisions. Having been to deaths in each of the terminals, of those arriving, in transit and departing, business travellers and those on holiday, passengers and staff, it is sobering to see how the reality of eternity removes distinctions that during our lives can seem so significant.

Those from virtually every country pass through. There are vast differences in the economic circumstances and purposes of these journeys. But they all use the same relatively small bits of concrete to take off and land.

It is a privilege to seek to serve whoever is in front of us irrespective of the multitude of differences, knowing that God's love is truly universal. It often feels like we are "watching the world go by" and it brings home with freshness one of the most famous verses in the Bible: "For God so loved the world that He gave His only begotten Son that whosoever believes in Him should not perish but have everlasting life."(Jn 3. 16).

The questions people ask!

"Sitting among the teachers, listening to them and asking them questions. And all who heard Jesus were astonished at his understanding and his answers."

(Lk 2. 46,47)

The Lord Jesus set an interesting example when, at the age of twelve and recorded in Luke chapter 2, He listened, asked questions, and gave good answers. Years later His public ministry had plenty of those three. He patiently listened and gave remarkable answers. He also used the asking of thought-provoking questions to lead the listener into truth. Even in the routine interactions we have with people, I think it is a useful example to seek to listen well, answer wisely and ask insightfully.

I am happy to share the most common question I am asked as a chaplain. If you are now holding your breath for some profound theological conundrum or philosophical insight into the human condition, I'm afraid you may be disappointed!

I think "Where are the toilets?" would be the strongest contender!

I've never understood the more worrying variation, "Are there any toilets here?"! (It would be a significant design shortcoming if there were not – and mean a quarter of a million people walking around the airport each day with crossed legs!)

The variety of vocabulary for this most universal of needs is an interesting reflection of attitudes across different cultures. I have never known urgent hand signals fail to convey meaning in this context, even when spoken language has proven insufficient!

We do have to be quite strict with some questions. "Can you look after my trolley while I go to the bathroom?" is not actually a question we would ever answer in the affirmative. While it may feel a little bizarre taking a baggage trolley to 'the little room', they are of course designed space-wise with that in mind.

A stranger question came from the minicab driver who asked if we would look after his car while he went to avail himself of the facilities. The restrooms are not designed to take vehicles, in the way they are for trollies, but we did not fancy explaining to the police why we were babysitting his taxi - and I don't suppose the driver would have appreciated us taking it for a drive. Some brief directions to the car park and the driver was fine!

"What is a chaplain?" or "What does a chaplain do?" is a sufficiently regular question that I have some standard answers that help the conversation flow on spiritual things. (This is continuing a practice I started as a young Christian. I have found it useful - in the spirit of 1 Peter 3. 15, "Always be prepared to give an answer to everyone who asks you to give the reason for the hope that you have" - to have some thought-through answers on key aspects of faith).

Not everyone needs to ask what a chaplain does – and when someone is aware of the role of a chaplain, it often indicates that they have a military background or have worked in an environment such as prisons or health care where chaplaincy is common. Sometimes this gives opportunity to speak about subjects they have previously discussed with a chaplain in a completely different context, and it feels like the words of the Lord Jesus in John 4. 38 when He said, "Others have laboured, and you have entered into their labour." It is truly remarkable the way God brings people into contact with those who will talk about spiritual matters at different points in their life.

I remember a day that a profound question came at a moment's notice. I was nonchalantly walking through a quiet Terminal 5C and was barely conscious of an elderly couple coming up the escalator from the track-transit system (this is the automated train-like vehicle that shuttles between the A, B & C buildings of Terminal 5).

"There is someone who will know," I heard, and as I turned round made a pre-emptive mental note of the location of the nearest toilets.

"Please can we ask you a question … we have something we would really like your help with?"

Perhaps they have a medical condition that means they are desperate I surmised!

"What will heaven really be like?" came the enquiry.

Now I am ready for virtually anything as a chaplain, but that did take me back a little and I think I replied along the lines of: "That's an interesting question… is that where you are hoping for a flight to today?" That at least gave me a little thinking time!

As part of giving a more considered reply, we talked about the difficulty of explaining flying to those who have never seen an aircraft and how that, for most of human history, what we today consider as routine would have been thought of as utterly impossible. In much the same way, we shouldn't be surprised that the Bible says relatively little about heaven. It is so outside of our human experience that detailed explanation would likely just generate as many questions as it answered. Yet, while there is so much that is difficult to explain to someone who has never experienced it, flying is a source of enjoyment to those that have. God gives us plenty of indication that heaven will be wonderful – by explaining what will not be there of our current experience (tears, pain, death etc.), and then speaking of how we will be with Him.

It is a prerequisite to being a chaplain that one does not "judge a book by its covers". A slightly impatient businessman had gone out to the lounge in Terminal 5B. This is not a problem (and if someone prefers it, they are welcome to do so). But the best route for returning to the A building as a departing passenger is not completely intuitive and involves a 10–15 minute walk (I have done it at significantly different speeds depending on whether someone is trying to catch a flight!). The gent was clearly used to "short and snappy" answers and having exhausted my normal repertoire of ice breaking and bridge building questions, I had pretty much given up on the conversation turning onto spiritual things.

Out of the blue he said, "So the difference between Christ as the Son of God and Christians as sons of God – how would you explain it?"

The pressure was on – and I never was any the wiser as to the reason for his question. I succinctly articulated the differences as best I could. He nodded, smiled, and said, "Interesting talking to you," and with that disappeared off to his flight.

Questions are a powerful conversation starter, and over the years we have learnt that all it needs is the right question to help people talk. A favourite approach of mine is to offer to walk someone to their gate. It saves attempting a complicated set of instructions (which may have to go via the vagaries of an online language translation service) and avoids the risk of finding the person an hour later still lost, and who then has less confidence in your ability to direct them than before!

Knowing the airport well is helpful in gauging how long a walk may be involved. A favourite question of mine is along the following lines:

"We have about 10 minutes to your gate. I'm a chaplain and you will probably never see me again. What would you like to tell me?"

I have lost count of the number of times when from behind a smiling and even confident face has come evidence of a burdened and often traumatised heart that is only too grateful to have someone who will compassionately and patiently listen. In a hurting and imperfect world there appears to be many people who, if given the opportunity and confidence to be vulnerable, are only too grateful to speak of their sadness, fears, pains, and perplexities. There is rarely anything I feel I can do to practically help improve the situations described but there appears a value, and sometimes even a relief, in them just unburdening the matter.

The area by the boarding gates in Terminal 2B gave an interesting question.

"Please help me chaplain," a middle-aged man asked. He was flying with his 12-year-old daughter and seemed quite agitated.

"I am not at all sure what to do and a chaplain is the perfect person to help me ... please tell me ... should I get on this plane?"

I asked for the man's boarding card thinking it was a rather emotional way to check if he was at the right gate. It was then that the penny dropped. The airline concerned was receiving extensive media coverage due to one of their aircraft disappearing into the Mediterranean Sea the day before.

"I don't want to die chaplain ... is it safe for me to go on board?" he said.

Now, much as I have considered myself to be a reasonable student of Biblical eschatology, he was giving me a dilemma. I had no more insight into the recent accident or safety record of the company concerned than anyone else and, with boarding closing in a few minutes, there was limited opportunity to explore the reasons behind his fears. I was also keen to ensure that if he decided not to travel - and there was the inevitable delay while their bags were offloaded – the decision would not be attributed to me.

I enquired as to why he wished to travel to his destination.

"I have urgent business to attend to," he replied.

"And does your daughter wish to travel?", I asked.

"Of course," came back the reply, "she wants to be back with her mum."

"So, what are your options?", I gently asked.

"Well, I can get on the aircraft, or I can walk I suppose," he said with good grace.

"And which do you think your daughter would prefer?", I asked as I caught her eye.

The two of them set off briskly to ensure they made the gate in time … but not before he had expressed his appreciation.

"Thank you, chaplain. That really helped," he said.

I was glad he thought so! Maybe it was just taking the time to let him know someone cared? It illustrated an interesting balance that I am sure many others in pastoral work have found. People's feelings are clearly important - but so too are facts. There have been many times when the operational imperative means lengthy debate is not possible - and in wider life so often there is not an unlimited time to talk. An yet a bit of time listening, explaining things slowly and reflecting to people using questions how they need to decide from limited choices can be helpful. Questions are helpful both ways!

I often think of Job in the context of questions, the book in the Bible with the largest number of them. God listened patiently as deeply-felt questions on suffering and difficulty were debated. At the end of the book there is not a list of answers but a series of bigger questions that God asked Job about the divine character which gave him a thoroughly different perspective. The ultimate reality is that God is far greater than us. And it is a paradox that through trusting Him rather than understanding our circumstances we can have hope. To have answers in life we must be thinking about the right (and perhaps much bigger than we normally ask) questions.

Never work with animals or children?

"Jesus said, 'Let the little children
come to me'."
(Matt 19. 14, NET)

There are many TLAs (Three Letter Acronyms) in aviation and even a few AFLAs (Alternative Four Letter Acronyms)! One of my favourites at Heathrow of the three-letter variety has a Biblical connotation that I suspect was entirely intentional. The ARC – or Animal Reception Centre – located on the south of the airport does a remarkable job processing the multitude of animals that travel through Heathrow. Pronounced "ark" it is a reminder of the large boat build by Noah as told in Genesis 6 and, as with many things in aviation, alludes to nautical travel in a by-gone era.

The pets and other creatures passing through the ARC have rarely requested the services of chaplaincy, but I have sometimes reflected on how it illustrates an important point. Vets and other animal welfare specialists would not come to mind when thinking of roles at an airport – and they are not those with whom passengers typically interact – but that does not take away from the significance of their role.

"I never knew there was a chaplaincy," is a comment we hear from time to time. With so much going on in the "city" that comprises a large international airport, that perhaps, is not surprising. Indeed, there are many specialist roles where I have heard people say, "I never imagined there would be one of those at an airport."

That relative anonymity stands in contrast with the way society sometimes uses public profile on social media as a marker of success. While being visible is undoubtedly important for some roles, there are many situations in the service of God where a willingness to quietly get on with the work without fanfare is crucial. The examples of Naaman's servant (2 Kings 5) and Paul's nephew (Acts 23) illustrate how 'big doors of consequence swing on seemingly small hinges of faith' and where the individual is not named or really known.

While chaplains have limited contact with animals, the opposite is true of children and young people who are a daily part of the airport, especially during the school holidays.

The point at which someone changes from being a child to an adult is a sore subject for anyone who, like us, has travelled with four offspring – as it is from age 12+ a passenger is considered an adult insofar as fare calculations are concerned!

The level of maturity and experience of flying can vary considerably between young people. A confident but very young-looking teenager asked me for directions to the business class lounge in Terminal 2. I asked where his parents were to which he cheerfully replied,

"O they are in Japan at the moment."

I checked his boarding card and sure enough he was travelling business class to Tokyo. Before I could ask more questions, he politely apologised and added:

"I do this trip on my own several times a year, commuting between my private school here in England – but I haven't used this airline recently."

I pointed him in the right direction and, with a slightly wry smile about the world of paradox in which we live, wondered how many other young people would have that as their pressing concern for the day!

It certainly stood in contrast with a school group I met who were on a charity organised exchange trip from a less privileged part of the world. In moving around the airport with them, it was necessary to use the rail network to travel between terminals. As they stood excitedly on the platform, one of their questions caught me by surprise. It was only then that I realised that having been on an aeroplane for the first time overnight to travel to the UK, this would be the first time most of them would have been on a train. How easily we take routine things for granted!

Judi is particularly capable with young children, and we have spent many happy hours walking around Heathrow together making the lives of families passing through the airport become significantly more peaceful and pleasant. A little time, a smile or a sympathetic conversation can go a long way to reducing the panic or stress level of adults in an unfamiliar environment trying to look after several little people, knowing this vacation is meant to be a relaxing break from the pressures of day-to-day life. It sometimes seems true that holidaying with toddlers is little more than paying to move the chaos to a different location!

During one of our earliest shifts together, we came across a lady with twin toddlers and a significant amount of hand luggage. We were glad to help and between us and mother got children and baggage safely on board. When leaving the aircraft and walking back up the airbridge, a man stopped us and to the amusement of the other passengers waiting to board said, "So is that what chaplains do all day ... help babies onto aeroplanes?"

As we smiled, he then added much more seriously – "Tell me, what do chaplains do?"

I was able to explain - and answer other questions he asked, including some specific spiritual ones about what motivates us to do the work. As a few minutes later he thanked us for stopping to talk and we walked away, I realised the other passengers had carried on listening. This experience has been repeated over the years - one person asking several questions and others being curious and listening into the answers. We leave it with God as to who He may be speaking to and helping in their spiritual journey.

Occasionally we have vouchers or gifts to give out and we will take every opportunity to tell families about the extra facilities the airport has to make their journey more enjoyable. We may offer to help push a trolley for parents who have run out of hands and for example in Terminal 5 say something along the lines of:

"Don't worry, after security there is a parent sanity restorer."

"I beg your pardon?" they may reply.

"There is a play area by Gate 2 and it is next to a coffee shop!" we explain which invariably brings a mixture of relief and laughter.

There is however a much more serious angle to children being at an international airport. Safeguarding is never far from our thoughts and being alert for the possibilities of trafficking, neglect, being taken overseas for forced marriage and a range of other issues are part of a role that is looking out for the good of others.

Lost children can present a challenging situation, and it is always heartening to see how many organisations quickly work together when it occurs. There are few feelings more heart wrenching than being with either a panicking child or parent when it has happened accidently, though the joy and relief when the situation resolves is great to see. God never loses His children (Jn 10. 28), but it has given me reason to reflect on quite how God must feel when we wander off and do not want to spend time with Him – and just how graciously willing He is to welcome us back when we have gone our own way.

Nervous passengers

"Do not be anxious about anything."
(Phil 4. 6, ESV)

I t might be expected that chaplains would deal with a lot of nervous passengers. Indeed, I suspect it is often a contributing but unspoken factor behind many of the emotions we see. But it is rare (in my experience at least) that someone seeks out a chaplain solely for that reason. Perhaps the real worriers never make it to the airport!

One of those times where someone did have reservations about flying, occurred when writing this book, and I believe illustrates the importance of being led by God's Spirit when seeking to do His work. Driving into the airport one chilly winter morning, various delays had occurred to my morning and, at the busy motorway intersection where my journey diverges depending on which terminal I am going to, I found myself in the outside lane. I had not entirely decided which terminal I was going to and so prayed to the Lord to be guiding my car tyres as well as footsteps! I was happy to be wherever He wanted me to be and felt at peace carrying on to the central terminal area and made my way to the chaplain's office in the prayer room of Terminal 3.

A small concern I had in starting to write this book was that it might reduce the time I had to be at the airport, but God had encouraged me on several previous occasions that He can guide someone to me just as He is able to guide me to them!

There is of course some understandable debate among chaplains as to the best way to operate. There is clearly benefit in being a mobile, visible presence "going out" to meet people where they are, finding those who would never think of seeking out a chaplain and being known 'around the patch'. There is also benefit in being in a set location where those that know about chaplaincy can find a chaplain and the quietness of a room can make speaking and praying easier. The answer is simple even if is not easy - and is the same for other decisions in the work of God: prayer and listening to the inner prompting of the indwelling Spirit of God.

On arriving at the prayer room, I noticed an older man head in hands. I enquired as to whether he was OK, he assured me he was - and shortly thereafter left. I finished my coffee and was about to open my laptop when he reappeared at the door.

"Actually, I'm not," he said.

It transpired that he was, in fact, feeling rather nervous about his flight that was due to leave in just over an hour. There wasn't long for a detailed conversation. We briefly discussed where he was going and the reasons for the trip. I gave some practical advice and, as he was happy for me to pray with him, I was glad to do so. He had some familiarity with one of the Psalms in the Bible and we talked about how that could be helpful to him. Then he was on his way.

The practical help we can give to passengers includes talking over just how safe flying is, and answering any specific fears passengers have. There are also breathing exercises that can help, along with distractions.

It has been a privilege to be involved with some of the British Airways "Flying with Confidence" courses at Heathrow, that over many years have been hugely successful in helping people conquer their fears.

Along with the practical advice, the spiritual part for me is also an important dimension. In the example above, it is powerful for that individual that God put the reassurance and help in place for him without me planning it – and indeed even me having reservations about whether an occasion sitting in an office was going to be a good use of the time.

Missionaries

"We departed and went our way;
and they all brought us on our way."

(Acts 21. 5)

It is a pleasure, indeed an honour, to be able to meet those who are engaged in serving in God's work from further afield and ensure that their transit through the airport is as smooth as possible. So often these are people who have made significant sacrifices for the good of others, and spend their lives in far less pleasant circumstances than they would otherwise have done. Often their work has a significant humanitarian aspect and there may be additional or unusual baggage to help with as they take materials not readily available in their location of service. Their journeys may also be necessitated by their own medical needs or bereavement, or because of war or persecution and involve traveling at short notice. Some of the remote locations where they serve mean their flights are part of a complex itinerary where disruption is more difficult to resolve.

There can be an almost overwhelming sense of change as missionaries first leave with youngsters in tow to head into a new country, culture and language as God directs. Conversely, those that are elderly may be returning to a country that has changed out of all recognition compared to the one they left. It may be difficult for those who have not had the experience to comprehend how a missionary feels when, with an increasing affinity and love for the people among whom they serve, leaving both their original home and their new home is hard – and something as simple as not being lonely at the airport can, we hope, be a blessing.

We were helping a Brazilian missionary couple recently. They were in transit from a conference in Northern Ireland to catch a flight to Sao Paulo with limited time and a terminal change to undertake. During their inbound flight, they had been talking to a pair of fellow passengers who had expressed concern about how they would find their way through Heathrow. Our missionary friends encouraged their fellow travellers to join with us and so, as a larger group than originally intended, we made our way smoothly across Heathrow.

The additions to our group spoke minimal English and were delighted to have guides - we did our best to look after them even though our verbal communications were restricted to a few online-translated sentences. One of the missionaries (who spoke Portuguese as well as English) was able to speak to them for much of the time and it transpired came from a similar hometown. I could follow nothing of what was said at the time but was interested to understand that a significant spiritual conversation had been possible. The missionaries took down their fellow passengers' details and planned to be in contact with them when they all arrived at their country of destination. I was also interested to understand by using a translation app that we were being referred to as "the angels" in their conversation!

Very often saying goodbye to the missionary is not the end of the story, as we have found God may be using their circumstances to put us in exactly the right place to have a helpful conversation with someone else. Late one evening, we had ensured some missionaries were efficiently on their way to South America. A couple of passengers waiting for the same flight were looking upset and it came to light that they should have been on another airline's flight to the same destination - they had just realised their mistake in misreading their boarding card. We attempted several options to resolve the situation before, ultimately, the decision was taken for them to stay in the UK for a couple of days. We organised reuniting them with their baggage and discussed the best way for rebooking their complicated schedule. As we waited with them for a relative to pick them up, kept them supplied with tea, and helped to keep them calm, they commented on just now timely and helpful our assistance had been for them.

Please ensure your own oxygen mask is fitted before helping others

"Come ... apart ... and rest a while."

(Mk 6. 31)

The words of the Lord Jesus to His disciples remind us that He understands our limitations, and, at times, rest is required. This is not to be idle but to be re-energised for future service. This chapter has been written to encourage anyone who cares for others – to remember that is not selfish to also have a care for ourselves.

Before I left my career in Health and Safety, it was becoming increasingly obvious that traditional injuries were a lot less common than once they were. Fifty years after the introduction of the Health and Safety at Work Act in 1974, the UK is arguably one of the safest places to work. That said, according to the Health and Safety Executive, one of the leading causes of workplace absence is "stress, depression or anxiety". Stress is a factor in almost everyone's life, and having enough to keep us working well but not too much that it does harm, can be a delicate balance.

The long-term psychological impact of COVID-19 will no doubt be the subject of discussion for years to come, although it may also be that an increasing willingness to discuss mental health related issues means there is some long term good for society from the experience.

At the most serious end of the spectrum there is the terrible statistic that, in the UK, suicide is the leading cause of death among men under 50, and in total over 100 people sadly take their own life every week (https://www.gov.uk/government/news/men-urged-to-talk-about-mental-health-to-prevent-suicide). According to cdc. gov, this figure is ten times higher in the USA.

Issues relating to poor mental health present a challenge for chaplaincy in at least three forms.

The first is the obvious likelihood that the people with whom chaplains come into contact can have any number of less-than-obvious issues affecting their mind – from an accumulation of pressures right up to serious mental illness - and a relatively minor matter at the airport can become a "flashpoint". Knowing that sometimes there is more going on when people are upset I said 'I can see you are having a difficult day....would you like to tell me what's been happening for you?' Whenever there is a disproportionate response to a situation, I take it as a flag to see if there is value in asking more questions. So often something has only been the last straw, and getting behind the presenting issue to the underlying cause gives an entirely different picture.

The second area of mental health is the wellbeing of staff. Different organisations favour a variety of offerings, but the wellbeing provision for staff is clearly an area where chaplaincy can feature if desired. Including contact details for the chaplaincy as part of signposting when difficult messages must be communicated, being part of internal roadshows, using the chaplaincy for advice on religious holidays, and giving space on the internal intranet are all options that can be used.

The third area (and which is perhaps least obvious) is the mental health of those who engage in chaplaincy – and in principle, anyone that is engaged in pastoral or caring work, whether formally in a church context, as a parent, or simple looking after others.

I sense that too often the commendable attribute of putting others first has been presumed to be mutually exclusive to looking after oneself. While a lack of care for others will prevent the *desire* for any good being poured out of our lives, it is also true that a lack of care for ourselves may prevent the *ability* to give to others. An empty container cannot pour much into another! Epaphroditus (Phil 2. 25-30) is described as near to death because of his exertion on behalf of others – and he is commended for that. However, the value of his long-term recovery from that experience is shown by Paul being grateful that he had now recovered.

Sacrifice of course has an important role in the Christian life, but we must be confident it is the Lord's will - being out of God's will and incapacitated is clearly detrimental to others as well as to ourselves! When the Christian life is pictured as a race in Hebrews 12. 1, it is to be run with endurance (or patience) – more akin to a marathon than a sprint! A long-distance runner may temporarily 'up the pace' but, for much of the time, keeping going at a rhythm that is sustainable in the long term makes the most progress.

Being open to the possibility of our own fragile humanity may sound like stating the obvious. In the cut and thrust of busy lives, the personal vulnerability to accept that God did not design us to work without rest, or carry more than He desires, can be easier said than done. Chaplains are not immune from either the volume or intensity of their work, and having those who can be empathetic or who will proactively 'check in' on how someone else is doing is essential. Likewise, the space for honest reflection with ourselves - or those with whom we can be open without fear – I have found to be essential.

Recognising the personal signals that our own body is flagging is essential. These may be general stress indicators (of which there could be many - from waking up during the night reliving experiences, to feeling sick, to experiencing anxiety). Others may be specific to the airport or chaplaincy (such as feeling physically drawn to previous suicide locations or vivid flashbacks from serious incidents).

While these will vary between people, I think there is value in every chaplain (perhaps everyone!) having their own 'personal care plan' that they have thought about in advance. Pressures can build insidiously and at the point where help is most needed, rational thought may be more difficult. Different people no doubt find different things helpful – and perhaps also different strategies for different circumstances – but knowing that there is always an option for support is critical.

These may include:

- Peer support – informally by debriefing each other or knowing who else on the team can be contacted. (TRiM – Trauma Risk Management - is a more formal version of this that can also be used.)
- Friends – Paul spoke of one who was a "true companion" and of others who "shared my struggle" in Philippians 4.3, NASB. This may sound obvious – but to gain the real benefits that come from having friendships where we can speak openly, time will need to be invested in them.
- Writing a shift log or journal – this may be therapeutic in processing what has taken place, as well as giving a record of events.
- Exercise - There are days when I feel content that I have had sufficient exercise as several miles can be walked around the airport without really noticing (it may be readily apparent the next morning!). Other shifts are more static. If you find having a leisurely swim gives a good time to pray, do it!
- An Employee Assistance Programme is standard in the wellbeing provision of many large organisations, and it has been good that the chaplains have had access to one at Heathrow for some time.

- Switching off - Finding the way that works personally so that we can 'switch off' despite the phone being on, is necessary, especially if there are extended times of being 'on-call'.

- Having some form of routine or repeated action at the start and end of the day may be important. During one of many online calls during COVID-19, I was involved in a wellbeing forum talking through with staff the issues they were finding especially difficult. A memorable quote came from someone who said how much they missed their commute! This caught everyone by surprise until they explained that having a time doing something different either end of the working day enabled them to segment their home and work life.

Genuinely taking matters to the Lord in prayer may sound like an obvious and important action – and so it is. However, I have not listed it first to make the point about balance. If we have a broken arm, prayer is essential - but it is not the only action to take. When Elijah was suffering (in 1 Kings 19), he spoke with the Lord and the response was both practical (with sleep and food) as well as miraculous.

When checking in for a flight, crew self-certify that they are, to the best of their knowledge, 'fit to fly'. Honestly checking we are sufficiently 'healthy to help' – physically, mentally, and spiritually – is part of acting responsibly. Appreciating when it is necessary to walk away from (or not engage in) a situation can take a lot of courage but is also critical for our own good and the benefit of those who are in need.

There can be an opinion formed when looking at some of the grand holidays undertaken from an airport, that because such trips away may never be experienced, that any break is out of reach. From time to time finding the right break away is nevertheless necessary -

and should be viewed as a helpful recharge for future service rather than as an extravagant luxury.

Emergencies

"The Lord will guard your going out
and your coming in."
(Ps 121. 8, NASB)

One of my favourite quotes from my safety career is "Living is incredibly dangerous - history indicates that out of the billions of people that have tried it, pretty much everyone has found it to be fatal!"

It is hard to convey just how amazingly safe modern aviation has become. In keeping with the adage "safety is no accident", the industry works to fantastic professional standards to ensure that each day over 100,000 commercial flights take place safely (www.aog.com). It has been estimated that at any given point in a day over one million of the world's population are airborne. It hardly seems possible that it was only just over a hundred years ago at the end of 1903 that the religious Wright brothers postponed their first flight (so as not to do it on a Sunday!) and the aviation industry was born.

That achievement forms an important backdrop in speaking about emergencies. So often dramatised in the media, I suggest it is important to keep a sense of perspective that both their frequency and severity is not likely to be best judged by reading a tabloid or social media. When significant events take place, there is plenty to be done as a chaplain – and it may make more interesting reading than the day-to-day walking around the terminals - however the frequency of these events is incredibly low.

There is always a chaplain "on call" 24 hours a day, although Heathrow is very quiet during the middle of the night. As a couple we are typically on call once or twice a week and if the airport control centre does ring, it will likely mean a passenger or staff member is either very unwell or has sadly passed away.

In addition to medical emergencies, we attend training exercises, very occasional serious emergencies and organise memorials for past significant events.

I have come to appreciate that my rational view of the (generally lack of) severity of an incident is not necessarily reflected in the perception of the travelling public. Tiredness, boredom, and a lack of information - all of which are typically experienced in the processing that takes place after an evacuation for example - can adversely impact the perception of what people have just been through.

An individual's circumstances can also have a significant role. One Sunday evening, a call came to activate a part of the emergency procedures. Being one of the people closest to the airport, it did not take long to arrive at the reception centre for those involved in the incident. Although it made the national news for a few hours, the reality for almost everyone involved was that it was a bit confusing and frustrating, or unhelpfully added time onto an already long journey. As we worked our way among the 150 or so passengers, one man was in tears and asked for prayer. I wondered what I needed to say by way of reassurance about the events that had transpired.

I enquired if there were other things contributing to his anxiety. It transpired that he and his partner had hurriedly left where they lived, and through a complicated journey were now in the UK - and urgently needed to be on their way. They were concerned for

Emergencies

the well-being of relative who had not been heard from recently. What for most people was a minor inconvenience, for this couple was the last straw in a heavily emotional situation. We were only too willing to pray with him, talk over what had happened and help smooth their onward travel.

Reflecting on the difference between how I may view an incident compared to someone who has never experienced anything like it before, I am reminded of the rather different view God has about the things that can easily worry me. To the God who controls the universe, nothing in my life is troubling, and yet He listens sympathetically to the concerns of my heart in prayer. Indeed, it is perhaps because none of it is large to Him, He says I may "cast all my cares upon Him" (1 Pet 5. 7). While I am glad that here we have a rota for those 'on call', it is a reflection on God's greatness that He does not sleep (Ps 121. 4) and when we call to Him, He will answer (Ps 91. 15).

73

Working with others

"Be kind to one another, compassionate,
forgiving one another, just as God in
Christ also forgave you."
(Eph 4. 32, NET)

A wonderfully varied part of chaplaincy at a large airport is the wide diversity of different roles with which we interact. I do my best to stay neutral between the various organisations and departments, but if I was allowed favourites, I suspect no one would begrudge me saying the airport paramedics would be one of them. Each terminal typically has a dedicated paramedic on-shift at any time on a pushbike – a CRU or cycle response unit. When the most serious incidents happen, I am always struck by the amount of resource they can call on that will go into saving one person's life.

We are always on the lookout for the bright yellow bikes. In my early days of chaplaincy, I observed that a disproportionate number of times I saw them was outside coffee shops. I have since learned that is not at all anything to be concerned about! We are always happy to assist and in many cases talking with the relatives of the patient is a significant help both to those affected by the medical incident and the professionals involved.

After one of the few occasions when our assistance was refused, we followed up a few days later to see what the issue had been. Alarmed parents had dialled 999 concerned about the slightly blue-tinged genitalia observed while changing their baby boy's nappy. I suspect it took more tact than medical expertise for the paramedics to explain that the UK was a little cooler than the warmer climes the passengers had recently arrived from - and an extra layer of clothing would bring about an excellent prognosis. Their assessment that chaplaincy was not required did not seem unreasonable!

On another occasion a petite but straight-talking paramedic was describing how their morning had only involved minor issues and for a small graze sustained by a member of staff admitted, "I prescribed a healthy dose of man up"!

However, being a single responder in much more stressful situations calls for a cool head and confident skill. I gained an insight into just how knowledgeable they are when I came across an elderly gentleman who was feeling unwell, having walked with his wife from Terminal 2. He had found himself out of breath and simply unable to continue walking. I found them in the subway close to the central bus station, rather perplexed as to what to do. I was concerned about his recent medical history and, not sure how else I would get them to move, rang for the medics. After all the standard observations had been completed, the ECG machine was pulled out of the significant panier of equipment the bikes carry. It wasn't long before the decision was made that, to be on the safe side, the gentleman would go to hospital.

While we were waiting, the paramedic asked if we wanted to know a bit more detail about what the ECG was showing. I know I did not understand all the amazing details we were regaled with about the heart from the ECG output, but I was certainly impressed - even if I suspect that the paramedic was doing it to provide a distraction until the ambulance arrived!

When the time came for me to head home, I reflected on the way that we marvel at the technology involved in flying, but our own bodies are even more incredible. Nobody suggests aircraft happened without designers, how much less could an amazing organ like the heart have happened by chance!

Consuming alcohol and flying are never a good mix. In the arrivals area of Terminal 5, I was concerned for a tall middle-aged man who was staggering around and gave less than meaningful answers to my questions. I convinced him to sit down while I summoned assistance. I explained to the paramedic that I thought that it might be alcohol related and, along with taking steps to ensure he didn't fall on us, various checks were carried out. She suggested I see if I could find some contact details for our patient. Fortuitously I was able to find a way to ring his wife at home and, with as much chaplaincy compassion I could muster, explained that her husband was a little unwell and being seen to by a paramedic.

There was a long pause before my thoughts as to whether I had failed to communicate in a sufficiently compassionate manner were interrupted by a loud frustrated voice.

"Is he drunk again?" the (presumably long-suffering) spouse enquired.

This helped with one problem – it added weight to the provisional diagnoses – while presenting another. This transpired to be a sufficiently regular occurrence that those at home were unwilling to come and collect the gentleman. Some persuasive calls to other relatives eventually prevented a hospital bed being unnecessarily occupied.

In Terminal 2 arrivals, Judi and I came across a somewhat comatose young man slumped over in a wheelchair. We were initially very concerned as there was little response to our attempts to rouse him. We called over a passing paramedic who, with the insight of regular Friday night shifts, checked the signs to indicate it was nothing too serious. His parting shot was to keep an eye on him and that when he "came to" he would likely be complaining of a sore head.

We eventually managed to get a fuller story out of the gent who was feeling "the worse for wear". Following a weekend in Dublin where he admitted a significant quantity of the local beverages had been consumed, he had caused significant embarrassment to his travelling companions by being repeatedly sick on their early morning return to London. They had abandoned him at the earliest opportunity, and he was now left trying to work out how to find his way home.

We fed him, gave him some help with directions and stayed with him until he was fit enough to resume his journey.

"Why do you do this?" he asked, "This is all my own fault - and I don't deserve how kind you have been to me."

This gave an opportunity to explain that we were no different to him! He was puzzled and I explained that we believe God has treated us far better than we had treated Him. Ruined by our own folly in sin, divine love has given us far more than we could ever have deserved - through Jesus Christ. To show a little kindness that reflects the love shown to us is the least we could do. Through some tears - and no doubt a still somewhat fuzzy head - a look of understanding and appreciation came as we explained that while God may disapprove of things we do (even more than our friends), His grace is so sufficient that none are too bad to be outside of the possibility of His forgiveness.

15 15 15 15 ✈

Airport angels: a reluctant moniker

"Do the work of an evangelist."
(2 Tim 4. 5)
*"God sent you to be an angel
for us today."*

It was a normal Thursday morning for me. For a family who were just completing security in Terminal 5, it looked stressful. A misunderstanding about timings means they have come to the airport later than they anticipated and there is now just thirty minutes to go before their flight is due to depart. Three young children, two parents, two grandparents, a push chair and several bags make up the party - and now some liquid paracetamol needs an additional security check.

I ask some friendly questions to understand their situation and reassure them their gate is just a few minutes' walk away. I offer to stay with them and walk them to where they need to go, and they start to noticeably relax. Some smiles with the children and a conversation with one of the adults about the church they go to changes their focus away from the tension they were feeling. We walk to the elevators, tell the youngsters that pressing the right button is their test as to whether they will be able to help the pilots, and the adults breathe a sigh of relief that there is no risk of getting lost while they are with me. It is not long before I am bidding them a good flight as they join the tail end of the boarding queue. In among the looking for their travel documents, one of them turns and says with heartfelt appreciation, "God sent you to be an angel for us today."

I have lost count of the number of times I have heard this said. In the early days of being on the airport chaplain team, it felt strange to hear people referring to chaplains as angels. In my mind wings belong on aircraft and a halo is presumptuous for those only too mindful of their own short comings.

My view has changed over the years to at least accept the description – not because my theology has moved on the issue, but because of the instinctive way people have used the description. It is not just because of being kind and helpful, but rather that the timing of our presence and ability to resolve an otherwise overwhelming issue has given people a sense of the divine. Especially poignant have been the occasions where the individual has said they had prayed for specific help in the situation. I have come to see how appropriate, in some senses anyway, a term it is: heaven-sent, just in the right place at the right time and with a divine message.

The first language of the New Testament was Greek, the language from which many English words derive. Angel, meaning messenger, is one obvious example - with the Greek word being *angelos*.

With the prefix *eu* that means good (as illustrated in words like eulogy, meaning a good word, or euphoria a good feeling) having become *ev* in translation, it is straightforward to see that that evangel – or evangelist – is a good messenger, with a connection to the word angel.

Just as an evangelist is different to an angel despite the origin of the name being linked, so likewise as a chaplain I am not an angel in the true biblical sense despite the way many people use the expression. And yet it is hard to ignore that people clearly seem to recognise at least some similarities.

We live in an age where messages are continuously being

communicated to us. I heard a gentleman come out of the airport toilets recently singing, "All you need is love". I was slightly puzzled until I realised that this was the music playing inside the facilities! I presume when he came to fly, or look at his salary, he would agree with me about the short comings of that message – but it illustrates how easily (and perhaps insidiously) concepts can be being put into our minds.

It is bemusing that those with no specific theological knowledge seem to have a good idea about what an angel will be like! In my chaplain capacity I don't preach in the traditional sense, but there is nevertheless a message of good news. Many times, when the circumstances arise, there is clear opportunity to talk about the greatest of messages when people want to, and they express their appreciation for the conversation. Other times there is opportunity to explain a specific aspect of divine truth in response to a query asked.

Among the sound of hundreds of take-offs and landings, the bustle of many thousands of passengers and staff at Heathrow each day – people hear a clear message. God has given them a sense that He cares about their stresses and wants to remind them of spiritual reality by providing one of His children at just the right time into their situation.

16   16   16   16 ✈

Mistakes & shortcomings

"If we say that we have no sin, we
deceive ourselves."

(1 Jn 1. 8)

One of the interesting indicators of the divine origin of the Bible is that its narratives have nothing of the human tendency to present matters in a better light than reality. Famous characters and God's people down the ages are described as the flawed and imperfect servants they are.

When describing God's work, it is perhaps tempting to focus only on the good aspects. Written missionary reports by their nature must be selective, and it is understandable that when giving a verbal update, those who are speaking focus on what is encouraging rather than detailing problems.

A downside to this is that it can be tempting to feel one's own area of activity must be in some way deficient because it is never all 'plain sailing'. Just as turbulence is natural and safe when flying, so some lumps and bumps along the way should be seen as completely normal. Likewise, just as we expect to not learn everything on day one of doing a task, so there will inevitably be mistakes and experiences to learn from.

With 200 gates at Heathrow, it is sadly inevitable that just occasionally someone is accidently sent the wrong way. On one occasion I was in a hurry to get somewhere and was interrupted by a passenger wanting to know their departure gate. Without thinking I looked at the internal operational system we have on our phones and told the passenger where the aircraft was parked.

About an hour later they saw me again and said:

"Excuse me, I never did find that gate."

I double checked their flight details and then realised my mistake. Whereas normally the aircraft parking place and the boarding gate are the same, that is not always the case. This aircraft was parked on a "remote stand" (one not connected to the terminal by an airbridge) and the passengers would be taking a bus out to the aeroplane. I apologised and there was enough time to redirect them to the correct place – which they, perhaps surprisingly, still trusted me sufficiently to head towards!

Sometimes bloodshot and teary looking eyes are mistaken for more than the person just having been awake for twenty-four hours without their usual food and sleep. It is maybe surprising, with the volume of tired and upset people we speak with, that more are not cross.

I do remember one person that was rather frustrated. It was early on in my time as a chaplain and, when I came across them, they were distressed. I wanted to help but was unsure what I could do for the passenger.

"Do you have a tissue," they enquired.

"I'm sorry I don't," I replied.

"Well what use is a chaplain without tissues," came the withering reply.

A packet of tissues has been carried ever since and is one of several items that I have learned the hard way to have in my jacket pocket!

A more profound occasion when (in a light-hearted way) I was told:

"Well, you're no good as a chaplain," happened many years later in Terminal 5B.

Watching an aircraft prepare for departure, an older lady enquired as to whether I would be happy to fly today.

"Very much so I answered – I'm always very keen to go flying."

"So, you are not much use to me then," she said.

I look puzzled and asked what she meant.

Her thinking was that, as she was someone who was fearful of flying, I was of limited use to her as I could have very little empathy.

My gentle rejoinder was that if chaplains went around telling passengers they were personally scared of flying and would not want to get on board flights today, it might not be good for the airport's business, and we both laughed.

Very thoughtfully she then asked,

"So, tell me about a time when you are fearful – how does God help you in those moments?"

We were able to have a lengthy and meaningful conversation about the role of prayer, faith, the Scriptures, previous experiences, and the presence of God, and how they all help in handling the anxiety that comes to us all.

No one of us can fully experience everything that others go through, and I have found there is a lot of wisdom in normally keeping away from the expression "I know how you feel" - even similar sounding experiences may impact people differently. That said, what we go through is, in part, so that we can be a help to others. With a little honesty and lateral thinking, there can be many times when 2 Corinthians 1. 4 applies: "[the] God of all comfort, who comforts us in all our tribulation, that we may be able to comfort those who are in any trouble, with the comfort with which we ourselves are comforted by God." (NKJV).

Out of the hundreds of conversations I must have had with people at the airport, this is one I have not forgotten. Our fears – and our failures – can be quite personal, even idiosyncratic. We can easily assess the shortcomings of others through the prism of our own strengths, and wonder how an issue could possibly be a problem for others. If I can be forgiven for taking the verses out of their context and apply them more generally, the Bible speaks of how those that are strong are to help those that are weak (Rom 15. 1), and how those that are more spiritual will recognise when helping others that another day it may be them that need the help (Gal 6. 1).

The much misquoted and misunderstood "Judge not that ye be not judged" (Matt 7. 1) is not saying (as many seem to try to escape scrutiny by implying) that one must be perfect before they can correct or help another – that would be terrible. Rather there is no help possible if we are a hypocrite and struggling with the exact same issue. However, if we have removed the log from our eye, we are then able to help with the speck of which Jesus was speaking. This lady's willingness to recognise that it was possible for me to bring both my strengths and weaknesses into the conversation was refreshing and we both went away blessed from the interaction.

The essence of presence: an example

"I being in the way, the Lord led me."

(Gen 24. 27)

In principle, being an airport chaplain is not complicated. It is simply a case of being in the right place at the right time and saying (or doing) the right thing.

Now if only the practice were as straightforward!

There can be some human guidance given for what may be appropriate to say or not say – and perhaps more so for what to do or not do. There can be practical tips on "loitering with intent" or "walking with an interruptible plod", but there is no training guide for how to be in the right place at the right time.

However, that sense of right time and place has been at the heart of the presence aspect of my experience of chaplaincy. There are many times when the eerie precision with which a chaplain finds themselves present with someone in need has as much of a profound impact on the person being spoken with than the actual words said.

I am sure that different people would explain that precision in different ways. Is it just coincidence? I would say no. Instead, it is down I believe to a crucial and unseen part of a shift - that of prayer. Many times this has been done in the less than salubrious surrounds – said with no disrespect to the Heathrow facilities - of a terminal multistorey car park as we quietly pause in the car (and in the conscious presence of God) before entering 'the fray'.

An occasion that particularly sticks in my mind happened in Terminal 5 departures. I had only a few minutes earlier prayed for God's guidance before walking the short distance to the check-in desks. I found myself next to a young lady who was clearly incredibly distraught. It soon became obvious her situation was serious and a kindly member of staff ushered us away from the crowds and into an office where through the tears she told more of her story. She had come to the airport for an exciting holiday to take a break from a high-powered city job. While waiting in the queue, a phone call had brought the tragic news that a sibling had taken their own life. She was now concerned how to break the news to parents who were separated and one of whom had had a recent serious medical diagnosis. The confirmation we had taken her off the flight and would arrange a refund of her ticket was met with the merest of comment; the details of her dream trip dwarfed by what was now unfolding.

Tentative enquiries about anything spiritual did not seem welcome. It is a delicate balance in such circumstances to not in any way force the conversation, while recognising that it often takes a crisis for people to ask big questions about meaning and ultimate matters. Her unwillingness to really engage about spiritual things struck me as unusual, and later in the conversation the lady said she had grown up in a town in what had once been socialist East Germany and was adamant that no one there had even the remotest belief in God. As I spent the next couple of hours with her, she was under the impression that I had been called on a radio. When I explained that I just 'happened' to be there, it was the nearest I sensed to any softening of heart. Did I have any explanation for such a remarkable coincidence? Well, I explained, I had just been speaking with God and asked to be placed where I could be helpful.

Confident and articulate, she was able to discuss her views on a range of points despite her obviously difficult circumstances. But it was the reality of God at work through presence that was the only time I felt she seemed to really stop and think about whether there may be more to life than she had previously considered.

The essence of presence:
the Biblical background

"God with us" ... "I am with you always."

(Matt 1. 23; 28. 20)

One of the most well-known aspects of Christianity is Christmas – the celebration of the coming into the world of Jesus Christ. The name of the baby "Jesus" – meaning the Saviour – might be the most famous name in the whole world. God's purpose of redemption would be accomplished by the death and resurrection of the One who bears such a fitting name.

On the opening page of the New Testament, alongside the first mention of Jesus, we are introduced to another title that is equally significant – that of Immanuel, "God with us". Christ was more than a revelation about God - He is God Himself. God was not only providing salvation but came to do it by being present with us. While we can be in awe at the ways God has communicated – creation and the Scriptures for example are phenomenal – ultimately God spoke through His Son by being present with us.

Theologians refer to the communicable and non-communicable divine attributes – those that humans can exhibit and those that are entirely beyond us. Omnipresence is clearly only something a divine being can possess as an attribute, but that is not the only sense in which God is present. Air is 'omnipresent' is the sense it is all around us all the time - but most of the time we give it limited thought. Moving air is something we are much more aware of – from a draft to a hurricane. And then there is air that we specifically take into our lungs that keeps us alive. There are occasions and circumstances where the presence of God is manifest in a specific way. The divine desire to be present in a different way to omnipresence with those He loves is clearly something that is reflected in human design – most of us are sociable beings and appreciate the company of others.

I am grateful to those of my fellow chaplains with whom we have had discussions on the concept of "incarnational chaplaincy". As a Christian chaplain, I desire to show love and practical help, and indeed speak of salvation when appropriate, that is in a small way a reflection of the name Jesus. However, it is combined with, and done through, the agency of presence – and therefore seeks to also be a small reflection of the name Immanuel.

Tracing the presence of God through the history of the Biblical record

From a Christian perspective, God being intricately interested in His creation by being present with it, is a key Biblical concept - and is seen in every epoch of human history.

- In the Garden of Eden, God came to speak with Adam and Eve in the cool of the day. When it was spoilt by sin, they "hid themselves from the presence of the Lord God" (Gen 3. 8).
- When the nation of Israel had left Egypt, they were given detailed instructions for the construction of the Tabernacle. It was to be a sanctuary "that I may dwell among them" (Ex 25. 8).
- Solomon at the dedication of the temple said, in desire if not in reality, "O Lord, truly I have built a lofty temple for

you, a place where you can live permanently" (1 Ki 8. 13, NKJV).

- Christ is spoken of as dwelling among us (Jn 1. 14).
- When the Lord Jesus was leaving His disciples, a key promise He gave was that the Spirit of God would be present in His followers individually, "The Spirit of truth ... will be in you" (Jn 14. 17).
- Regarding collective gatherings of Christians in a church, the Lord Jesus promised, "For where two or three are gathered together in My name, I am there in the midst of them" (Matt 18. 20, NKJV).
- Regarding the future, the promise is made, "Behold, the tabernacle of God is with men, and He will dwell with them" (Rev 21. 3), and there will be the enjoyment of the name "Jehovah-Shammah", the Lord is there (Ezek 48. 35).

So, presence is integral to the history of God's dealings with humanity.

Presence is also a key aspect to the Christian's hope for the future. There is relatively little said in the Bible about what heaven will be like. This is understandable as our current earthbound experience makes understanding an entirely different domain impossible. A repeated theme of what the Bible *does* say is that it will be enjoying the presence of God.

For example:

- "I will come again and take you to be with me, so that where I am you may be too" (Jn 14. 3, NET).
- "Father, I want those you have given me to be with me where I am" (Jn 17. 24, NET).
- "Today you will be with me in Paradise" (Lk 23. 43).
- "Absent from the body ... present with the Lord" (2 Cor 5. 8).
- "With Christ; which is far better" (Phil 1. 23).
- "So shall we ever be with the Lord" (1 Thess 4. 17).

As many a traveller would attest, an enjoyable journey and a wonderful destination may be missing something: having those with whom they have shared the experience is often a key part.

Aviation facilitates people being physically present. The gloom merchants who foretold COVID-19 being the end of commercial flying, seriously underestimated both the legendary ability of the aviation industry to bounce back from seemingly existential crises – and more fundamentally, the social desire of human beings to be together. Online meetings have a great role – and many times facilitate what would otherwise not be possible – but can never fully replace the blessing of being "in-person" where that is an option.

I smiled recently with a frequently flyer who was explaining all the places they regularly visited on business travel for their organisation.

"What line of things are you in?" I gently enquired, knowing that many firms have looked to use technology to minimise travel as far as they can.

"Oh telecoms," came the somewhat paradoxical reply!

Presence is also the way God deals with His people today. There are no promises in the Bible that God will take away every issue (1 Cor 10. 12). However, in each circumstance there is His promise to be with the Christian (Heb 13. 5, Matt 28. 20). In the middle of a storm even the great apostle Paul was grateful that "there stood by me this night an angel of the Lord to whom I belong and whom I serve, saying, 'Do not be afraid, Paul'. "(Acts 27. 23,24)

"A ministry of presence" is a widely used expression regarding chaplaincy. It is certainly true that a chaplain does not always solve someone's problems, but they can be present and walk at least a little of the journey with someone. As such, chaplaincy can be seen as being in keeping with the Biblical understanding of the way God works.

No doubt the future will bring consideration of how far

'remote' chaplaincy can go. The chaplaincy website (www. heathrowchaplaincy.com) has proved helpful and effective as a means of contact in recent years. Having the ability to communicate with people when not physically present at the airport is important. Redundancy, furlough, part-time working, and time off for sickness are all situations when staff may wish to be in contact with chaplaincy – and online technology clearly facilitates that in new and useful ways. For some staff joining the workplace Bible study I have been involved with for many years, it may be easier when they are on an off day. For airline crew in a hotel 'down route', it can provide welcome fellowship at what would otherwise be a lonely time – and hence the use of online meeting software can be useful.

One of the more amusing changes to the airport post-Covid has been the addition of cleaning robots. These automated 'Dalek' looking contraptions can be seen in several passenger areas. Whatever they do for cleaning, they have produced an endless source of passenger entertainment, with conversations, smiles and photo opportunities. We have sometimes commented on whether the day will come that, with a yellow jacket or chaplain label, a similarly mobile device could ever do what we do. It would not suffer the pains or tiredness of the human body. But unless Artificial Intelligence one day has emotional sympathy or spiritual insight, the technology will have limitations - so for the near future at least I think the role of humans as chaplains is safe.

The theology of Christian chaplaincy

"But examine all things; hold fast
to what is good."

(1 Thess 5. 21, NET)

There are many important concepts that are not exactly referred to by name in the Bible but are readily observed with some careful reading. The Trinity is an obvious example! "Chaplaincy" is not specifically mentioned in the Bible. Nevertheless, if the basic concept is described along the lines of being present, doing good, listening and then - as opportunities arise - speaking of spiritual things, then chaplaincy is very much consistent with what the Bible teaches.

I have explained in the previous chapter why I believe presence is such a key concept in chaplaincy but there are other aspects I also see as consistent with Biblical principles.

1. Doing good

There is no question that the New Testament envisages a practical Christianity where generous kindness is shown to others. The Christian follows the practical example of Christ of whom it was said concerning His earthly life "all that Jesus began to do and teach" (Acts 1. 1). Irrespective of whether we see tangible results, the purpose of the Christian life is to glorify God by becoming increasing Christ-like – and He went about doing good (Acts 10. 38).

I readily accept that some people are more interested in practical good than spiritual blessing – but this is nothing new. It is at the end of the chapter describing the first miracle that we are told that Jesus knew what is in people (Jn 2. 24,25) and after perhaps the most famous of material provision (the so-called feeding of the five thousand, there may have been many more) it is obvious that some were there more for their stomach than their soul (Jn 6. 26).

It is quite clear that we cannot become a Christian by doing good – it is "by faith, not of works lest we should boast" (Eph 2. 8,9). However, as is so often the case, one Scripture is balanced by another nearby. Ephesians chapter 2 continues regarding those who become Christians that they "are his workmanship created in Christ Jesus unto good works that God has before ordained that we should walk in them." (Eph 2. 10).

The Lord Jesus did not expect all His followers' good to be done behind closed doors. Self-promotion and attention-drawing to our good deeds is of course unseemly and unspiritual, and drew the understandable condemnation of Christ (Matt 6. 1-4). However, "that they may see your good works and glorify your Father which is in heaven" (Matt 5. 16) indicates it is perfectly possible to be known for doing good in such a way that it results in glory to God.

There is clearly much more to the Christian life than doing good, and ultimately there is no point in a merely better dressed or better fed soul going to an eternal hell. However, in the Biblical picture of evangelism as seed sowing, it can be easy to merely bemoan the hardness of heart of many in their attitude to spiritual things. It seems consistent with the way a sovereign God works that He may be using the good done by His people to 'plough the ground' so that the seed planted, either contemporaneously or later, falls into softer soil.

The recipients of the Christian's good are clearly identified in Galatians chapter 6 that says, "to do good to all especially those of the household of faith". The early disciple Dorcas (also known as Tabitha) was a commended example, being full of good works (Acts 9. 36).

In the words of the old hymn:

> *Lord I want to be a blessing to someone today,*
> *Just a smile perhaps will do, To help them on their way,*
> *To maybe lend a helping hand, Or a kind word to say,*
> *Lord I want to be a blessing to someone today*

2. Listening patiently

While appreciating that all the Bible has value as the inspired Word of God, there are some passages that seem to stand out as particularly beautiful gems. The Lord Jesus joining two disciples on the Road to Emmaus (in Luke 24) is, I expect, a favourite of many Christians. Despondent and sad, their hopes dashed by the crucifixion of the Saviour, they were joined by the Lord who drew near and went with them. Some simple questions got them talking and the Lord Jesus just listened. The remarkable patience of the Lord Jesus is seen in His willingness to wait the right time to speak, knowing only too well the transforming effect His words would have.

In a similar vein, the delay in John 11 is initially surprising. "Lord behold he whom You love is sick" (v3, NKJV) was the desperate message from the distressed Mary and Martha concerning their brother Lazarus. When later than hoped the Lord arrives, the sad observation is made, "Lord, if You had been here…" (v21, NKJV). Yet now He was there and despite knowing that Lazarus' resurrection would very shortly follow, He patiently spent time listening to both sisters unburdening their hearts.

The sense of patiently and quietly spending time with people is seen in the events recorded in the chapter following this great miracle when another occasion at that house in Bethany is described. There is no fanfare with a crowd rehearsing one of the greatest miracles ever done - instead in John chapter 12 the Lord is reclining at the table enjoying a meal with Lazarus.

3. The guidance of God's Spirit and joining on a journey

My favourite passage in relation to airport chaplaincy is the journey in Acts chapter 8. Philip the evangelist was led by the Spirit of God to leave the preaching he was undertaking in Samaria to go and speak to a single individual. At the point where he set off, he did not know the details of the person God wanted him to speak to. After following the initial guidance, he was then specifically led to an Ethiopian. This man was an international traveller undertaking a long journey home, using one of the fastest modes of transport of the time.

Despite being well connected, having a good job and perhaps being outwardly religious, he appears to be searching for something more. Unable to comprehend the Scriptures he was reading, he invited Philip to sit with him on his journey for a while. The man was converted, baptised, and then went on his way - and they never saw each other on earth again.

Perhaps one of the most well-known "journey passages" in the Bible is that of the Good Samaritan (Lk 10. 25-37). The Lord Jesus spoke of a man travelling on the arduous trip from Jerusalem to Jericho. An unexpected problem occurred: the man was attacked, lost his money and nearly his life. Whether the story was true or a parable we are not told, and it does not matter. While there are great pictures in these verses of Christ and the work of salvation that He has done, we cannot escape the simple lesson about doing good to foreigners on a journey with an unexpected problem despite their inability to repay or the likelihood of seeing them again.

4. Trusting God to work

While completing this book, I had reason to be studying the book of Esther. It is famous for the name of God not being explicitly mentioned. The nation of Israel was also hardly at its spiritual peak. Yet in those difficult days, God was clearly still at work: it is certainly true that while His name is not heard, His hand is clearly seen. One of the book's most famous verses is when Esther is reminded that it is "for such a time as this" (Est 4. 15) that she was where she was. Simply being available in the right place at the right time and doing the right thing furthered the purposes of God, saved many, and was for the blessing of God's people.

The book of Esther must obviously be read in the light of the rest of the Bible regarding practical living, and is clearly not intended to be a textbook for mission. But it is a poignant reminder that God has people in places to accomplish His purposes – divine workings do not necessarily coincide with human predilection on methods.

While writing this book, I was in a coffee shop many miles from Heathrow, typing away while Judi was shopping. Through a set of circumstances, I found myself in meaningful conversation with someone nearby about spiritual things, the unusualness of which spoke to the person. Afterwards another adult, who I had not really realised was listening, told me that they were a relative and had been praying for that person's good for many years. They had been encouraged to keep on doing so from listening in to the way the conversation had happened.

Just as with Esther, even where circumstances do not look favourable spiritually, God can be at work. Even in secular spaces, those that are willing to be courageous for God and follow His leading may have the privilege of seeing divine overruling and something accomplished in the purposes of God.

The business of chaplaincy

"So then, as we have opportunity,
let us do good to everyone."

(Gal 6. 10, ESV)

However valid the theology for chaplaincy, by nature it operates in a secular space. There is therefore a 'permission to operate' that at the very least must be implicit within its context. Several types of chaplaincies (and airport chaplaincy is an obvious example) are within the setting of a high security environment, and that permission must be explicit through the granting of access. I expect that in the future, an increasing proportion of Christian work that has historically been undertaken informally in secular spaces may be done under a chaplaincy umbrella – and so long as that brings good governance, rather than unreasonable restriction, that has the potential to be mutually beneficial.

Due to that need for 'permission to operate', the benefit of the chaplaincy therefore must be obvious to the organisation - and there is a variety of ways in which this could be expressed.

Most organisations have a financial driver of some description – whether it is to generate profit in the commercial sector or at least to achieve a budget. There may be the potential for chaplaincy to highlight a contribution to either increased revenue or reduced cost without that becoming a primary factor. In previous roles I did, safety was recognised as having some intrinsic value, but it was also true that often "good safety is good business" and in some contexts it was useful to demonstrate this.

While it is ideal to be able to express business benefit in quantitative terms, this would not be entirely expected in an area like chaplaincy. Indeed, at the other end of the spectrum, there are many things that even businesses do because they are the 'right' thing to do rather than for direct financial gain.

Enabling staff to do their role

There are times when chaplaincy 'frees up' members of staff to do the job they are paid to do.

When I was a very new chaplain, I was perhaps too willing to do this! A significantly inebriated passenger was giving some staff a dilemma. She clearly wasn't fit to fly (it is never a good start when that is obvious at check-in!). Letting her wander around the terminal wasn't a great option. Putting her into a hotel to come back the next day seemed unreasonably generous – and could make the situation worse. At that point I was passing … and an enterprising member of staff came up with an idea.

"Chaplain, can you help us here please?"

I politely enquired as to what he had in mind.

"Please bring this passenger back in time for the last flight to Madrid this evening sufficiently sober that we accept her for travel."

Much as I knew the Bible has plenty to say about not being drunk, I wasn't sure it had much guidance on how to handle the situation, but I could see any theological protestations were unlikely to be effective!

I spent a tedious couple of hours persuading the passenger to drink as much coffee as I reasonably could while listening to her ramblings. At least she was safe, and it wasn't tying up other staff! With my patience wearing thin I was very relieved that when I took the passenger back (and with a bit of coaxing to ensure she did what she was told) she was accepted for travel.

A more recent example happened in Terminal 3 landside departures when Judi and I came across a paramedic attending to a lady in her early twenties. The passenger was uncommunicative and rigid in her limbs, a panic attack in full swing. After her key signs had been checked and a bit of history eventually gained, the medical options were limited. Helping the person with her breathing and being reassuring, eventually got her to the point where she could talk. There were other urgent calls for medical help coming over the radio and we offered to stay with the passenger. The paramedic was confident there was no other medical concerns and appreciated our offer, then left to care for another more seriously ill patient. With time and controlled breathing, the person eventually told us more of her story.

They were finishing a course of study with important exams, and the previous day there had been a terrorist attack not far from where she lived. Her flight had been delayed, she hadn't eaten and was now concerned about her delayed long-haul flight which could mean missing an important family occasion. After a while, we were able to give her something to eat, let her offload how she was feeling, ensure she was routed in a way that would get her home in good time, and gave reassurance of where she could get help if anything unexpected happened. By the end of our interaction with her, she was really relaxed, unnecessarily apologetic and more than able to continue her journey.

Preventing use of resources

On an occasion in Terminal 5B I recall working with a passenger to help a teenager who was very upset and starting to panic. A staff member was alarmed and quickly on the phone to airport control to organise an ambulance. We made progress with the individual and were able to have the staff member end the call with the promise that we would call for help if the situation deteriorated. The situation passed, and the youngster was contentedly readying herself for boarding when she turned to myself and the other person who had given assistance and said:

"Please can I have a selfie with you?"

We looked at each other with that "Yoof of today" type expression that tries hard to resist the rolling of eyes - until the young person explained.

She had these episodes quite frequently and often people were really kind and supportive - and so had a habit of taking a picture with them.

"When I feel the world is against me," she said, "or I worry if I will cope in the future, I scroll through my photos and am reminded of all the caring people I have met."

She showed us her album of kindly strangers and we were of course happy to oblige.

Every time a paramedic or other staff member is freed up, a delay is prevented, overnight accommodation is not necessary, or service recovery averted - is the double win of a happier customer and less cost for the business.

Good customer experience

It would be entirely understandable if, after a particularly difficult experience, a passenger chose to fly through an alternative airport to avoid painful memories. This however gives an opportunity: to particularly care for someone during a difficult time. A colleague had been with a passenger when her husband had died after a long flight from Singapore. As we often do, he finished the time with the bereaved relative by offering that the next time she flew through the airport, a member of the team would be willing to accompany her. This serves several purposes: we can see how they are coping; we can distract from the memories that may be present; and minimise their stress if it is difficult. We often find, in practice, they have also reflected on spiritual matters in the meantime and are in a much better place to speak than in the immediate circumstances of a crisis.

This proved to be the case in this instance, and it was a privilege to speak together with the passenger. When I asked how she had found coming through the airport this time, she poignantly replied that the quality of care she had been shown during one of the worst days of her life meant she had no qualms about coming back. Compared to someone avoiding a location for years afterwards or feeling very nervous each time they came through, this is an excellent outcome for the individual, but also the business.

With the vast numbers passing through Heathrow each day, chaplains cannot hope to help even one percent of travellers – but we can make a significant difference to a few. A passenger in a wheelchair was being pushed along by his wife when I met them in the baggage reclaim area of Terminal 3. They had experienced various difficulties with both their flight and the airport. I was able to significantly calm them down and explain the various processes that would be involved in sorting out their issues. By the time I had walked with them out of arrivals and found a taxi for them, they were feeling decidedly better about their day. When one of them said "you were the best part of Heathrow", it made me stop and reflect. There are so many capable individuals and a huge amount of capital invested that makes Heathrow work - but what had made the difference to that couple at that point was some extra time and compassion.

There are so many times when a little time and care has elicited a response that shows we have clearly made someone's day. In a customer service business, these interactions are valuable and happen as a 'by product' of caring chaplains being present.

Facilities and values appreciated by stakeholders

Any respectable business in aviation puts considerable thought and resource into the practicalities of ensuring safety is a key priority and managed effectively. That must be tangible, firmly based on evidence and lead to desired outcomes. What may be much more nebulous is how to make a passenger feel safe. There is no true benefit to society in 'smoke and mirrors' that merely makes someone feel safe while the underlying risk management is rotten. Conversely the business does not gain the full benefit from the investment in safety if the end user does not feel as safe as they truly are.

"I feel safe because you are here," has been said to me on numerous occasions walking around the airport. I will confess, perhaps because of my background, to being especially committed to doing my bit for safety, but it is minor compared to the significant expertise that goes into the risk management of aviation. But I am very happy to help people feel safe and hope by my presence and regular prayer for the industry to be a contribution.

While the benefit may not be appreciated by all, those of faith will be glad to know that chaplains regularly pray for the airport and the wider aviation industry. This includes for safety for those travelling, for peace, and for wisdom for those making significant decisions. God never promises to take away difficult circumstances, but I firmly believe that prayer makes a difference as we navigate the challenges.

As a chaplain I obviously do not always agree with all the commercial or operational decisions taken – but if truth be told I am more frequently glad to not be the one having to take the decisions. Agreement is also a different matter from, particularly in times of crisis, giving messages of support to those in senior leadership. The assurance, to those having to take decisions that will impact thousands of people's lives, that we as chaplains are praying for them rarely elicits anything other than a grateful message. I never yet heard "I really wish you wouldn't do that"!

Multi Faith Prayer rooms are valued by a considerable number of passengers and colleagues around the airport, with ten currently provided within the terminals at Heathrow. Along with the goodwill they generate, these have several practical business advantages including improving the experience of the airport to those who do not wish to use them. Careful thought is required in their design and operation but ultimately where the provision is well done, it has the potential to influence both customer and colleague decisions that are also for organisational good.

Staff wellbeing

In contrast to those who pass through once or twice a year, for thousands of people the airport is their place of work. While it may be a place associated with the excitement of exotic holidays, for colleagues the airport is the place where they bring the ups and downs of day-to-day life. It is a privilege over time to get to know them and, when someone feels the need to offload or to come for a longer chat, be available to contribute to helping with their wellbeing. We are privileged to be able to mix with staff while they are in canteens and rest areas and the sense that someone cares can be a help to somebody's day – even a smile among the busy pace of a shift can help reset perspective.

One day I was sitting quietly in one of the staff areas of the airport and a slightly flustered looking pilot sat down nearby. After a while I enquired as to whether he was OK. He was having a tough day and explained he had failed a part of the process for becoming a captain for the second time. He felt it was unlikely he would be given another opportunity and the career limiting disappointment was obvious. I listened, and as he appeared open to further conversation, I gave the example of how I had benefited growing up in a home where a pilot career was balanced with other priorities and how promotion is not everything. We talked about what really matters in life – and death - and then my own motivation for having left a career in aviation to be engaged in Christian work. He seemed to appreciate a timely conversation and I hope there was lasting benefit.

Another day while mixing with some cabin crew, one appeared a little nervous and confided that they were concerned about being lonely while away from home in the location to which they were travelling. Their attention had been drawn to our chaplain jackets and it transpired they attended a church in the local area. They were very happy when we prayed with them and they went on their way feeling very different about their concerns. We were able to put them in contact with a crew manager we knew from the staff Bible study who stayed in contact with them during their trip.

These are examples – there are many times when staff make a passing comment that shows they really appreciate having chaplains at the airport with the listening ear and wider perspective we bring.

Measuring and communicating benefits

With a small team and the more significant engagements with those that we help often being quite lengthy, it is inevitable that measuring the benefits of chaplaincy is going to be about qualitative as well as quantitative factors. The adage of "You can only manage what you can measure" can only go so far in a work that is fundamentally spiritual in its character.

Quantitative measures can include:

- Days (shifts or hours) given to the airport by chaplaincy. This could be expressed as a financial equivalent using a nominal salary / employee cost.
- Number of visitors to prayer rooms
- Emergencies and number of responses to more significant incidents

- Services held – whether religious or memorial in nature
- Complaints handled – chaplains are uniquely placed to help with those that have a religious aspect.
- Facilities faults, or near miss reports relating to security and safety
- Website visits or other recordable tangible engagements that can be tracked over time.

Qualitative measures

- As will be obvious to anyone engaging with the Bible at even a superficial level, there is power in storytelling. This is important for chaplaincy as perhaps the most powerful way to illustrate the obvious help given to an individual.
- Keeping shift logs of some description is important for a variety of reasons including safeguarding and accountability. It also allows the many long forgotten happenings to be relayed.
- Passenger and staff feedback can be recorded, and having a mechanism where this can be done easily is helpful. Sometimes passengers will specifically ask where they can send in appreciation. Other times passing on a card with appropriate contact details so that they can be in touch in the future has the unexpected benefit of a complementary note being received.

Chaplains by their nature are normally content to work in the background, recognise that their contribution to the overall working of the airport is relatively small, and it is God that is at work rather than them. It can therefore go a bit against the grain to do the necessary work of publicising, in the right way, the good work that is being done. It wasn't always God's purpose to speak about what has been done (Mk 1. 44) but there is a Biblical principle that testifying to the good things that God has done is important (Lk 8. 39, Acts 14. 27). Finding ways to do this such as attendance at regular airport meetings, a space on the airport internal IT system, noticeboards, and news items helps maintain profile.

Personal relationships also play an important part. Having 'advocates' (those that understand and recognise the value of chaplaincy) within the airport management structure can be particularly helpful. This will take time and patience to develop but may also in itself yield opportunities for chaplaincy – a high power job is by no means insulation from family difficulties or spiritual questions for example. Trust, wisdom and 'professional boundaries' are all factors (as in any role) but the ability to interact at all levels within an organisation is an important component of the chaplaincy profile.

Where a chaplaincy is a charity, there is a legal requirement (in the UK at least) to produce an annual report - and such accountability for money spent is entirely consistent with Biblical principles. Producing a colourful, engaging, and informative document that outlines clearly what the chaplaincy does and that is suitable for wide distribution, and which includes some great stories, has proved effective in both raising profile and widening the appreciation for the work done. It is hard for those in need to contact those who can help them if they are unaware that they exist. As has been rightly observed, the time to get to know the chaplain is before you think you need them!

Practical models of chaplaincy

"And there are diversities of operations, but it is the same God which worketh all in all."

(1 Cor 12. 6)

While this chapter is quite specific to airport chaplaincy, I hope it illustrates a wider point. The individual context within which an individual serves can be influenced by many factors. A similar looking work may have the same aims and principles but be in a different setting and it will not necessarily be able (or be desirable) to be a clone of what is done elsewhere. The above verse, in its context, is referring to the different gifts God uses in a local church. However, it appears consistent with a wider Biblical principle – that while never changing in His principles and standards, God is characterised by beautiful variety not only in creation but in His works more widely.

Contact – and ideally travel - outside of one's "comfort zone" can quickly illustrate that a similar work may legitimately appear quite different elsewhere – and if that knowledge is used wisely it can be useful learning or cause for reflection. One of the benefits I believe of Christians maintaining a heathy missionary interest, for example, is to help them not be stuck in a personal echo chamber of their own local experience.

Aviation by its nature has had to be an increasingly standardised industry. From the (generally!) worldwide use by Air Traffic Control of English and the phonetic alphabet, to the mandatory safety briefing for departing passengers and the insistence of the use of checklists by crew, there is a recognition that safe travel between countries - with all their differences - does not happen by chance.

The aviation industry was not long born when it was recognised that having a way to deal with misplaced baggage was going to be necessary! While bag losses are statistically small, there has been an agreed protocol for managing matters such as lost bags since the 1920s. There are two organisations that have been instrumental in coordinating international air travel. ICAO is the International Civil Aviation Organisation and an agency of the United Nations, and IATA is the International Air Transport Association, the association that represents most of the world's airlines - and between them are responsible for a lot of the standardisation within the industry.

That sense of commonality does not apply to airport chaplaincy where there are significant varieties in the way things are organised, driven to some extent by the size and design of the airport, the sense of mission of those engaging in the work, their financial position, and the legal framework for charity style activity in their jurisdiction. I outline some of these below.

Shared prayer spaces vs faith specific rooms

Some airports have individual facilities for each faith group which enables personalisation of the rooms and makes holding faith specific activities easier. The airport design often means this is not feasible, and shared spaces will need to be blander, with storage space for individual groups. Protocols for use are particularly important where facilities are shared and will likely need pictograms to illustrate text where there are many international passengers.

Static versus mobile chaplains

Providing an office space near a prayer room or chapel means that a chaplain can be in a known place at a given time and speak with a degree of privacy with those who wish to do so. That space may need to move – airports are regularly constructions sites! – and seek to adapt to the changing 'people flows' as buildings and the industry changes. There are also benefits to chaplains being 'out and about' where those in need can be spotted, help provided where people are, and a high level of visibility reminds people about the existence of the chaplaincy.

Integrated with or separate to specific humanitarian work

Airports have a need to be working with a variety of government departments and charities – such as those providing housing for the homeless, assisting returning nationals from overseas, helping refugees etc. Some chaplaincies act as the conduit with local and national organisations, whereas in many larger airports there is a separate charity or department that handles this (but with whom the chaplaincy will likely work closely).

Degree of interaction with control authorities such as the police and immigration

Prison chaplaincy is a long-established and quite distinct area of ministry compared to airport chaplaincy. Airports nonetheless have a substantial police presence and will likely have custody provision close by – and there will be holding rooms as part of the immigration process. There are several ways in which airport chaplaincy can be involved – there are clearly synergies, and it may help add to the case for the presence of chaplaincy at the airport – while recognising the knowledge and resource requirements for doing this aspect may be additional to what is needed for the airport itself.

'Employment' structures

Chaplains may be employed by the airport, be employed by a charity directly tasked with chaplaincy at the airport, or employed by an organisation which seconds or loans the chaplain to the airport. Chaplains may also be 'volunteers' - who also come in a variety of forms such as retired, self-employed, faith-supported, self-supporting, grant/sponsorship funded, or with a separate job. The extent to which there is overarching leadership between religious groups can vary, along with the extent to which the airport provides any renumeration to those involved. It is essential that there are agreed and clear appointment processes, operating standards, and disciplinary procedures but which can accommodate as far as possible the diversity of backgrounds and circumstances from which individual chaplains may come. Practical matters around insurance, branding, expenses, and internal IT system access all need careful thought.

Public space vs private property

The legal status of an airport has a direct bearing on what activities are permitted, and who grants that permission. In some jurisdictions, free speech case law has led to "public booths" where virtually any religious organisation can engage in conversation with the public within the terminal building. In others, bylaws and private ownership completely restrict who can be on airport property to those with formal permission.

Despite these variations, airport chaplaincy has had an association for many years. The International Association of Civil Aviation Chaplains (IACAC for a necessarily shorter name!) exists to share good practice and helpful information, be a network to facilitate helping passengers along their journey, hold meetings and conferences, and be a place for mutual sharing and support. I have enjoyed serving on its board and look forward to helping it develop more ways to practically help chaplains.

I hope this outline of something of the diversity of airport chaplaincy I have come across encourages, and is interesting to those who have experience of it that is different to my own.

More broadly, if you are seeking to do a work for God, I hope you are encouraged to have faith in His leading (Rom 8. 14)! His Spirit will obvious never lead someone to act contrary to teaching that He has revealed in the Bible, but in practical matters Biblical history shows God is not limited to merely replicating how He has acted in the past or elsewhere. There is plenty to learn from the experiences of others, but as illustrated in the events in Acts 16 for example, there is a clear Biblical expectation that we genuinely seek and trust God's guidance for specific situations.

Interactions with other works

"All things work together for good."
(Rom 8. 23, ESV)

Judi and I have never managed to follow the advice "Stick to one thing". No doubt there are times when it is wise to ensure our limited time is not spread too thinly but the 'synergies' between our activities have turned out to be helpful. The chaplaincy has been combined with regular Bible teaching and preaching, visiting schools for assemblies and Religious Education lessons and hospitality. While these other works are completely independent of being a chaplain, in God's goodness these works have not turned out to be as disparate as it might initially appear.

On one memorable occasion, some pupils from a local school where we take assemblies came to a Christmas service at the airport chapel. It was an interesting venue for the youngsters to visit and showed a very different part of their 'neighbour' that they probably just associated with the aircraft flying overhead or a relative's employment. I like to think these community engagement opportunities can inspire the next generation to work in aviation - and hopefully also illustrated that faith is a part of the 'real world'.

A secondary school we know well had a school trip passing through the airport. It was well within our normal activity to accompany them, ensure all arrangements went smoothly, and the staff kept their sanity. It also acted as a useful illustration to the teenagers of the syllabus material about Christianity in the community. Similarly on a variety of occasions we have used the chaplaincy during RE lessons when we have been talking about the reality of following Christ and caring for others.

There have been many occasions when our general experience in education has been helpful when coming across school groups passing through the airport. We feel a certain admiration (and perhaps sympathy!) for teachers using their holidays to take young people away on an overseas trip. When things go wrong, schools normally have the support of a specialist travel agency but there are times when our knowledge is also helpful. A sadly memorable example was when I was asked to accompany a school group through arrivals where one of the young people had tragically died while they were abroad. No amount of time in school fully prepared for that, but experiences like this, I find helps my preaching stay mindful of the awful realities of life.

Bible teaching has always been a key part of what I enjoy, and I often find myself thinking about passages I am studying while walking around the airport - and being alert for relevant experiences. The use of a suitable story, appropriately anonymised, from the chaplain work when I am preaching, has sometimes then led to someone who has been listening, and planning on passing through Heathrow, seeking our advice, reassurance, or practical assistance.

The saying, "Strangers are friends you haven't yet met" is attributed to the Irish poet Yeats, and the Bible certainly encourages a kindness towards those we have not met before. In contrast to the familiar word 'xenophobia' meaning 'stranger fear', the word for hospitality in the language of the New Testament is '*philoxenia*' meaning 'the love of strangers'.

Hospitality is a work we feel is important and we have often been able to enjoy the mutual blessing that comes from doing this work in the various forms it can take.

While separate to what we formally do as chaplains, there have been many times when our familiarity and proximity with the airport has meant that during disruption to someone's journey, a mutual acquaintance has put those having a difficult day in contact with us.

We have found it a part of the wonderful blessing of being part of the family of God to meet for the first time those with whom we share plenty in common - and at times this has led on to further friendship or more opportunities to help others. In Romans 16. 2, Paul said to those in Rome to assist Phebe in whatever she needed. He could never have envisaged something like the printing of boarding cards or other needs connected with modern travel, but I think it is included! There are certainly many things that can be a reasonable application of the gracious words of the Lord Jesus in Matthew 25. 40 (NET), "I tell you the truth, just as you did it for one of the least of these brothers or sisters of mine, you did it for me."

We could never have predicted these relationships between the works when starting off, and yet God has a great way of integrating things when they are done in His will. This is not surprising for One who at a much grander scale "works all things according to the counsel of His own will" (Eph 1. 11, NKJV).

Epilogue – the journey

"Jacob said to Pharaoh, 'All the
years of my travels …' "
(Gen 47. 9, NET)

An unexpected benefit of chaplaincy is that one is rarely short of a metaphor! This has (I hope) enhanced my preaching, although that is perhaps as much for others to judge than me. Many times in the Bible – and particularly in the teaching of Jesus Christ – parables are widely used. Common items were referred to and simple lessons applied that made the listener think and made spiritual truths clearer.

In this closing chapter, I want to use a selection of the situations I come across at the airport that I have used to illustrate wider truth from the Bible, and that I have found helpful in either formal preaching or informal conversations.

Journeys have destinations

An international airport is a great place of journeys. And whether physically travelling or not (and indeed whether we like it or not!), we are all on the journey of life. Our lives, like journeys, have a beginning, middle and end, and while the exact length and nature of our life journey is unknown, the fact that it comes to an end – it has a destination - is starkly clear. It always surprises me that with all the preparation and thought we put into things in life, we don't pay more attention to where we are going.

When speaking with passengers I will often ask:

"Where are you travelling to today?" and it is rare that a definitive answer is not forthcoming!

Indeed, when someone is unclear as to where they are going it immediately gives rise to suspicion and further questions. There are plenty of passengers for whom trips have been a year or more in the planning. I find it staggering that so much forethought goes into an earthly trip without more planning being given to eternity.

There are some people who say regarding life "it's all about the journey" - and by that I presume they mean they want to enjoy the experience as much as possible. With some things there is certainly more than one way that can lead to a similar outcome in life. However, it is obvious that for most passengers it is about rather more than the journey. In fact, quite a number give the impression that the journey is an inconvenience, and they are just looking forward to reaching their destination!

On one occasion I was having a discussion with a traveller in her twenties, and she was quite dismissive of my suggestion that we should be paying more attention to where we are going than the experience of getting there. So, I asked for her boarding card and suggested we try an experiment. I would also ask several other passengers for their boarding cards, mix them up and hand them back randomly. After all everybody would get a similar experience of going on board a flight.

"You can't do that," she said with a smile, "you'll cause a riot!"

And so I suggest it is with life … people will put up with all sorts of difficulty to reach the right destination. I have lost count of how many times I have calmed down a stressed passengers by encouraging them to focus on the beach or mountain they will be experiencing in the near future - and the present difficulty will be a distant memory. It hugely matters about our life destination – especially when, according to the Bible, we will be there eternally.

I have found it profoundly challenging each occasion I have been at the scene of a death where someone was desperately trying to reach a specific destination to die. Laden with medical drugs and paperwork - and often acting against advice - they have endeavoured with tremendous effort to reach a different part of the globe to die. Even more poignant for me than the obvious sadness of the circumstances, has been wondering whether they put as much thought and effort into where they will spend eternity.

Security

While I have no scientific study to quote, I have a level of confidence that the number of people who identify passing through security search as the favourite part of their day, is reasonably small. And yet we do it. And some of us do it several times per day. Whether we agree with - or even fully understand - the rules, we submit to the scrutiny recognising that there are those who have made rules to whom we are in subjection. I am no exception - as a chaplain I am subject to the same standard and prohibitions. It is similar with God's presence. Far greater than an x-ray machine or metal detector, the Bible says "all things are naked and open before Him with whom we have to do" (Heb 4. 13).

All are subject to a gaze that penetrates beyond human understanding. On several occasions I have observed security finding items that a passenger (or on one or two embarrassing occasions even myself!) had forgotten we were carrying. It is sobering to think of God knowing the wrong things I have long hidden away from my memory.

The Bible is clear for the future, that regarding God's presence "there shall by no means enter it anything that defiles ... only those who are written in the Lamb's Book of Life" (Rev 21. 17, NKJV). The standard is universal and the scrutiny perfect. When explaining security processes to new chaplains I do warn them that using the technically correct nomenclature of "clean" and "dirty" to refer to whether passengers are "screened" or "unscreened" may lead to some strange looks! It would not go down well to say to someone, "You need to come this way as you are a dirty passenger"! It is a great truth that the Bible says regarding Christians, "the blood of Jesus Christ His Son cleanses us from all sin" (1 Jn 1. 7). It is one of the many great paradoxes of the gospel that the God who knows our faults the best, was willing to find a way to deal with them.

A place of faith

Most people readily appreciate why - in a place where there is a wide spectrum of human experiences, significant emotion and sometimes stress - there is an obvious need for chaplaincy. It has been a rare occasion in over ten years of chaplaincy where someone has passed a negative comment. One time was when a passenger – I think in a somewhat inebriated state - said we shouldn't have people of faith in secular spaces. I smiled at the irony. Thousands of people every day put their trust in what is unseen (the power of air) to support them as they make journeys that for almost all human history would have seemed laughably impossible. In a small tube, 6 miles up in the sky we hurtle around at three quarters of the speed of sound, in an atmosphere where we cannot naturally breathe, surrounded by temperatures far below freezing. We can do it for hours on end – and pay for the privilege! Pilots and cabin crew, designers and engineers, air traffic controllers and airport staff we have never met, work together to keep it safe - and in some instances very much have our lives in their hands. When we consider the remarkable levels of trust being exhibited, I sometimes wonder whether airports are a place of greater faith than many religious buildings!

Many times, people understandably ask questions about the difficult experiences they or others pass through. Flying reminds us – as do natural relationships and even the use of the unseen in our human body – that faith enables us to experience more than we can fully explain. Our understandable quest for answers to problems and suffering should be with the purpose of gaining greater knowledge to grow and inform faith rather than replace it. Even the most brilliant aeronautical engineer must still be prepared to trust the unseen if they are to experience flight.

Faith is different to feelings. I am sure not everyone shares my tingle of excitement as the aircraft speed builds along a runway as part of take-off, but feelings are not what makes flying happen – joy, peace, anxiety, and apprehension are probably being felt by different passengers on every flight. Rather it is being willing to trust something more powerful than ourselves that enables us to benefit from it.

Faith is also different to action. The inability to contribute to the Christian's standing before God is made clear by several Bible verses, such as Titus 3.5, "Not by works of righteousness that we have done, but according to His mercy He saved us". It is aptly illustrated by considering the hypothetical situation where part way along the runway during take-off, a concerned passenger flaps their arms to the best of their ability. No useful lift is contributed in the slightest - however hard they try – and indeed their furious efforts are likely to both tire themselves and give others reason for concern! It is not a reflection on their lack of effort but rather that as human beings we are not designed to generate lift. Likewise, by our nature we are completely unsuitable to do anything to get right with God and the Bible says we must depend entirely on Jesus Christ who said, "Come unto me ... and I will give you rest" (Matt 11. 28).

Resurrection

I have often found that when we have a holiday planned, we

will end up meeting passengers who come from, or have travelled to, that part of the world. It is particularly insightful to find out about a place we have not previously visited by speaking with those who either live there or at the very least have passed through. It therefore stands to reason that if Jesus Christ came from heaven and rose from the dead, He is uniquely qualified to tell us about the character of heaven and what happens after death. When we were planning to visit Australia, we had great advice from those who could say, "I am Australian." On the greatest of journeys, I do not think there can be a greater guide than the One who said (and later proved), "I am the resurrection and the life" (Jn 11. 25).

Guidance and direction

I consider it an absolutely privilege that a total stranger will relax and come with me when I offer to show them the way. They know little about me, I do not bore them with my years of experience or give them a complicated set of directions. Nevertheless, they normally stop looking at the signs and accept that so long as they stay with me, they will be fine. I will answer questions but there is not normally time to give them several hours of explanation and even then, it would likely just lead to more questions.

There is nothing more frustrating than someone taking a wrong turning thinking they know best or spreading doubt in the minds of others as to the right way to go. If they are simply willing to follow where I am leading, they will reach their gate in good time, we will have enjoyed a chat about anything they want to discuss along the way and they will often say, "That was a relaxing journey though the airport, but we could not have done it without you."

I challenge myself to be as content in my life to simply walk in step with the One who is the perfect guide, in keeping with the famous words David said many years ago, "The Lord is my shepherd, I shall not want." (Ps 23. 1)

Time critical

I frequently deal with those who are concerned about time.

To stand by an empty gate a few minutes after a flight's departure with a flustered passenger hopefully asking, "Can you do something?" with their aircraft disappearing into the distance is an almost surreal experience! The excuses are many.

"It's only a few minutes."

"It's not my fault."

"I was tired with my journey and fell asleep."

"I was enjoying the lounge too much."

"We were still packing this morning and left late."

(And that is not to mention those who have clearly spent too much time in either the bars or the shops!)

Then there are others at the opposite end of the spectrum – they are very organised and the moment the gate is displayed they go into such a panic they cannot think straight enough to follow directions to go the correct way!

A less well-known part of the Christmas story concerns a man called Simeon who said, "Lord now you are letting your servant depart in peace ...For my eyes have seen your salvation." (Lk 2. 29,30, NKJV). In a similar vein, Paul wrote with anticipation in 2 Timothy chapter 4 "The time of my departure is at hand." When the moment came, they were both not only ready but could also "depart" the journey of life with peace.

Arrivals

My favourite place to watch people is international arrivals. There is plenty of joy, hugs abound, and there is a constant supply of smiles. My interest in aircraft notwithstanding, there are times when I look at the happiness from people being together and give thanks for what aviation makes possible.

There are balloons and banners, placards, and pets - and often a palpable sense of the anticipation of meeting. I particularly like the way that it is very public. No one is ashamed that they are there – nor do they care what others think.

One couple took that to an extreme – and, along with dog, came all three in full Santa Claus outfits to shamelessly meet a couple of timid looking teenagers in Terminal 3. With total disregard to the obvious chagrin of the poor young ladies, I watched as the mother laughed and said in a very loud voice, "Well we thought it was funny!"

Many people sadly seem adversely influenced worrying about what others will think, but a moment after Christ returns, the Christian will have no regrets about having been seen as odd by those around. No wonder Paul was willing to say, "I am not ashamed of the gospel of Christ" (Rom 1. 16).

The preparation 'Meeters and Greeters' make is sometimes remarkable. Late one night, I found a young man loitering in a corridor by the central bus station. When challenged, he explained that his girlfriend was arriving from the USA on a flight into Terminal 2 the next day. I checked the details and they appeared to be genuine. My update on the flight's expected arrival time just underlined how long he would be spending on a less-than-bed-like seat in arrivals. I wished him well and went on my way - challenged by his willingness to endure a night of discomfort in anticipation of the one he wanted to see. The spiritual application of enduring the difficulties of the spiritual night is easy to see with the soon return of Christ being anticipated.

Home time

And then everyone is gone. There is something quite strange about staying until all the flights have finished and seeing the familiar buildings virtually empty, devoid of the throbbing life of the teeming crowds. All the excitement and activity of a large international airport can overshadow the way that, for most people, their visit is very transient. Soon they are on their way – home and hotels replacing boarding gates and baggage carousels. The temporary nature of both the airport and the longer journey are quickly subsumed into the fabric of wider life. Sometimes at the end of a hectic day I look around a now almost eerily quiet terminal building and really wonder where everyone has gone!

However long the journey is looked forward to, and however complex or exotic, it is eventually over. And so it will be with our lives – one day the journey will have passed and be gone. We will look back and in the words of the Bible, "You do not know about tomorrow. What is your life like? For you are a puff of smoke that appears for a short time and then vanishes." (James 4. 14, NET).

What destination are you headed to? How confident are you of reaching it? Jesus Christ said, "I am the way the truth and the life" (Jn 14. 6). If you have never trusted Him as Saviour, I hope you will do so today before the journey is over, and know heaven will be your eternal destination.

For my fellow Christians, I hope you feel encouraged to make the journey count. To seek to be in the will of God, live for the good of others and see God work for His glory - a privilege truly above and beyond.